Also by Kathy G. Widener

Where Memories Live
The Return Home
The Southern Child

Every Life Tells a Story

Every Life Tells a Story

KATHY G. WIDENER

Deeds Publishing | Athens

Copyright © 2021 — Kathy G. Widener

ALL RIGHTS RESERVED—No part of this book may be reproduced in any form or by any electronic or mechanical means, including information storage and retrieval systems, without permission in writing from the authors, except by a reviewer who may quote brief passages in a review.

Published by Deeds Publishing in Athens, GA
www.deedspublishing.com

Printed in The United States of America

Cover design by Mark Babcock.

PAPERBACK ISBN 978-1-950794-53-9
HARDCOVER ISBN 978-1-950794-54-6

Books are available in quantity for promotional or premium use. For information, email info@deedspublishing.com.

First Edition, 2021

10 9 8 7 6 5 4 3 2 1

'This is dedicated to the one I love'
My Husband, Jimmy A. Widener

"A happy marriage is the union of two good forgivers."
— Ruth Graham

Contents

Storytelling...An Art	ix
Introduction: The Rest of my Story	xiii
1. Beginnings	1
2. School Begins	9
3. Seventh Grade	17
4. More Room	21
5. Christmas 1962	25
6. On the Road Again	29
7. Vacation Time	33
8. 1965 School and Big Changes	41
9. Fireworks for Life	45
10. Courtship	51
11. Basketball Games and Honors	57
12. Young and in Love	63
13. Senior Year	69
14. Our Wedding	81
15. Marriage, Living on a Shoestring	85
16. Motherhood	91
17. The 1970's and Style	99
18. Snowstorm of the Century	105

19. A Son is Born	111
20 Wisdom Comes with Age	117
21. Partying at a Beach House	123
22 Brush with the Law	127
23. Camping in the Smokies.	131
24. Back to the Past	137
25. Events to be Remembered	141
26. Teaching by Example	153
27. Then Along Came Baby	159
28. Another Precious Life	165
29. Remembering Those Who Went Before	171
30. Sights and Sounds of Washington D.C.	177
31. The First Time I Ever Flew	185
32. Back to School	191
33. Crossing the Pond	197
34. Austria in Spring	203
35. Small World Connection Stories	211
36. Summer of 1999 — Love and Lost	217
37. Into the Twenty-first Century	225
38 Daddy Could Tell Stories Too	227
39. She's Gone Now	231
40. Glimpses of a Life Well Lived	237
41. Time Passengers	241
42. Advice From My Lifetime	245
About the Author	265

Storytelling...An Art

I think of my Grandma's homemade patchwork quilts, patterns and colors, the hues of the rainbow. Sometimes, her quilts were cutout shapes that formed patterns, stars, or overlapping rings, mostly just cloth scraps cut square or rectangle, no special pattern involved.

Growing up, our old clothes were recycled for her quilt making. Swatches from my brother's shirts covered with cowboys and Indians were some of the oldest. Pieces of dresses, skirts, or blouses we girls once wore. Seeing these small squares remind me of stories associated with these fabric pieces.

Grandma never wasted anything. Her family lived as poor tenant farmers growing up and as an adult surviving the Great Depression. She learned to be very frugal. Never discarding the last little wormy apple in the fall, cold rice, or leftover biscuits. She saved everything that she thought could be used and repurposed later. I guess I get that trait from her, the saving part, not the repurposing. True Southerners seem to find it extremely hard to discard significant reminders of their life.

The homemade quilts that belonged to my Grandma, probably made generations before, are now family treasures. Crocheted throws, blankets, and doilies, all made by hand, even handkerchiefs in all shades and patterns carried in Grandma's apron pockets. Sometimes they also had embroidery in the corners, or a small slice of lace.

Southern writers are very passionate about the past. It is complicated. The people of this region have lives, seemingly lived in layers that could be peeled back like an onion. An astute listener is soon exposed to the why and how their culture developed so differently from any other sections of America by the stories they tell. There is always the misunderstanding that Southern writers have to concentrate on poor, racist, and anti-intelligent people, which is absolutely not true. The mistaken notion that Southerners are not highly intelligent may have some small part in our melodious accent. That slow southern drawl can be smooth as silk and sweet as honey when it falls on the ear of any southerner who comes back home from another region or country. Maybe our accent is derived in part because we grew up with hot, muggy summers when the temperature and humidity seemed to force us to move at a slower pace. We had to conserve our energy, play and rest in the shade when possible, gulp glasses of cool spring water or sweet iced tea, taking frequent breaks. I am not saying all Southerners are intelligent, by no means. I have some suspect relatives and have met my share of Southerners that are 'a few sandwiches shy of a picnic', if you catch my drift. What I really hate is when major news networks pick the Southern woman with curlers in her hair and front teeth missing to answer the question, "What did the tornado sound like?"

"Breathes there a southerner without a story to tell? One of the oldest pastimes in the world is the art of storytelling, and yet it has survived every modern invention that vies for our leisure time. Southerners love to hear a good story, but more than that – they love to tell one." (Grissom, Michael, *Southern by the Grace of God p.* 379). I can never forget the interesting stories that I was told. I continue to pass these down to anyone willing to listen when the direction of a conversation reminds me of an entertaining person I've met, a place visited, or an experience remembered. These stories also extend to knowledge shared by family, friends, and acquaintances, their stories.

There have been many storytellers from the South of the highest caliber, geniuses at weaving tales, true and fictional. The greatest Southern novel of all time is considered by many to be *Absalom, Absalom* by William Falkner (Mississippi). He also wrote short stories; *"A Rose for Emily"* is one of my favorites. Then we have Margaret Mitchell's, *Gone with the Wind*, the only novel she ever wrote. It is a wonderful, complicated tale of the antebellum South. Miss Mitchell was born in Atlanta, Georgia. She reportedly said, "I was ten years old before I realized that General Lee and the Confederacy had lost the War." I had heard it said, the book is usually better than the movie and, in this case, it definitely is. I have read *Gone with the Wind* three times and my oldest daughter is Melanie. Sounds almost like an obsession. Right?

There are, of course, many great storytellers born and steeped in the South, almost baptized in sweet tea. Robert Penn Warren (Kentucky) wrote *All the King's Men* about the consummate politician Huey Long from Louisiana, Thomas Wolfe (North Carolina) *Look Homeward Angel* was loosely based on his own families' experiences and of course *To Kill a Mockingbird* penned by Harper Lee from Alabama, a great tale of injustice righted by a brave and determined lawyer, Atticus Finch.

These great storytellers were very influenced by their Southern roots. My writing is intertwined with my Southern roots, I mean literally. They are memories I personally have stored in my memory bank of my experiences; or tales told on the front porch in the moonlight from rocking chairs my Granddaddy built during the 1930's.

To be a good story teller, you need to tell a story in such a way that the reader can experience it first hand: visualize the oranges and pinks of the sunset, smell the sweet scent of roses or honey suckle wafting on the night breeze, hear the sizzle of chicken dipped in flour and frying in a black iron skillet, or the sound of rain falling, splashing on leaves or the roof above. All these stories describe in vivid detail my family and the life we lived.

Storytelling is a skill most Southerners are born with. It is reinforced by their childhood experiences; especially my generation that grew up in the 1950's and 60's with strong traditions and family values. Church on Sunday mornings and company visiting on the weekends, sitting around in the living room or on the front porch conversing and catching up with family news. I consider myself fortunate that I was raised to be independent and had family to depend on for advice, love, and discipline, if needed. To my wonderful family and the love and support they gave to me, Thank You! Most of all, thanks for the storytelling.

Introduction: The Rest of my Story

Sometime at night, I lay in my bed awake, my mind is cluttered with memories. I can remember so many things that have happened in my lifetime, even I am befuddled. How can I remember so much about the distant past, but have to concentrate to remember what I did last week or even yesterday? I guess, as we get older our short-term memory gets shorter. My thoughts are cluttered with the past. Metaphorically, it is an attic full of treasures, things that I can envision keep running through my mind. There is no sleeping; my mind is too awake. I can see faces from my youth, colors of clothing that others and I have worn and people from fifty years ago, their faces I probably would not recognize today, but I can see what they looked like when I was a girl.

This tumbled, cluttered attic of memories needs to be organized; each memory written down. Even my life has been a story. We all have stories and they need to be shared. Someday, when I am only a memory, my descendants will, hopefully, appreciate my storytelling and descriptions of what I have witnessed, shared by the written word. Simple everyday occurrences begin to be important with the passage of time. Cobwebs hang suspended from the rafters in this imaginary attic, misty opaque webs, like hopes and dreams, some fulfilled, others linger only in my mind. How can these memories be explored unless I record them? There are trunks, boxes, and other clutter just waiting to be opened.

In one corner of this cluttered attic, my girlhood, teenage years repose. The fashion trends we all followed, people, places, and events that I can relive in my thoughts. I imagine basketball games, cheerleading in front of a crowd of enthusiastic fans, the wooden gym floor waxed to perfection, reflecting our movements, the walls reverberating with our voices. There are memories of riding a school bus each day, fifteen miles one way, to attend classes and to away basketball games with coach, players, and the cheerleading squad. After home games, there are visits to Bo's, a local teen hangout, occasionally sock hops were okayed by the Principal, Mr. Nichols. We were gyrating teenagers moving to the music and dancing to the twist with Chubby Checker. My personal favorite was Dee Dee Sharpe's 'Mashed Potato Time'; which inspired a great dance, the Mashed Potato, of course.

Our music was furnished by a record player spinning our favorites. No street shoes allowed, only stocking feet, thus the name sock hop. Songs by the Four Seasons, the Beatles, the Monkees or the Rolling Stones blasted through the air. Slow songs by Elvis, Bobby Goldsboro, or B.J. Thomas when sweethearts slow danced, holding each other close, concentrating only on the here and now. Being young and having a special someone was everything then. There were cakewalks at the harvest festival, sleepovers and parties; fun things I did with friends. 'Those were the days, my friend, we thought would never end', but they have. It's been a revolving door; seasons come and go and getting old comes so fast. I now realize that youth is truly wasted on the young. I know, I've been there.

The classes I took, Science and Biology under Mrs. O'Daniel, Band under Mr. Helms and of course English under Mrs.

Robinson. She didn't put up with any nonsense, but I like to think she would be proud of my writing. The one course that I appreciate now, typing under Mrs. Snelgrove, the only subject that turned out to be beneficial. She also taught me shorthand, a total waste, and bookkeeping. Miss Doris Gunter taught Home Economics, no longer required in public schools. At that time, the 1960's, girls were taught how to run a household. There were few opportunities for females besides housewife, teacher, or nurse, not to diminish these occupations in any way. There is no higher calling than raising children with manners and common sense and being able to run a household. Teaching students our country's history and how our nation was born and the sacrifices America's founders made are the basics tenets for our freedom. Of course, the knowledge of the nursing profession is a precious gift, a healing touch ministers to not only the body, but also the mind of the sick and disabled among us. Running a household, teaching children, and basic health care should be considered life skills, not just for females.

In Miss Doris' class we learned how to sew, which I did use later, meal preparation, and how often we should change our underwear. We could have figured that out on our own. Miss Doris was something of a prudish lady, never having been married, she definitely did not speak about relationships with the opposite sex. That was a taboo subject to Miss Doris, also a product of her time. When reviewing my old report cards, Miss Doris had given me low marks in conduct because I talked too much in class, imagine that. Piled on top of these girlhood, high school memories and observations of my surroundings, are the happiness of becoming a mother and the sadness of losing those dear to my heart.

Trunks full of pictures, scrapbooks, and all the memorabilia of a lifetime crammed into old dresser drawers. A cedar hope chest given as a gift when I graduated from high school contains too many crazy things to mention. Why would I hang on to 45 RPM records, greeting cards older than all my children, and letters my husband and I wrote to each other over fifty years ago? Peeping into my hope chest recently, I discovered my marron high school sweater, my name stitched in gold thread on a tag in the back, K. Gantt. Even my shoelaces of the same hue that I laced through my white canvas tennis shoes are still there. We kept these canvas shoes bright, not by washing, but by polishing with white liquid shoe polish. I have so many stories, and I am miraculously able to remember events and circumstances that most people have long forgotten.

I have not done great things in my life, but I have met some truly amazing people and have had opportunities to hear and witness people's actions, travel to places and experience things others only dream of. The most amazing people were those I grew up with. My Grandma Florence, born in the Victorian era, 1887, had a gentle spirit and the patience of Job. My Daddy, a wise man, with his mother's kind and calm temperament, who loved and cared for us. Daddy kept all his school books from his high school years. He graduated in 1940 from Fairview High School with thirteen students in his class. They actually took a Senior trip to the Mountains of North Carolina, a place we visited many times in my youth. I have the pictures from their Senior trip in Daddy's scrapbook. There are many pictures of my siblings and me growing up. He also, evidently, loved taking pictures. Just recently, I discovered his graduation announcement with the names of his Senior class. His geography book, American History book, and his Economics book now reside on my bookshelf. He signed his name on many pages and wrote 'begin and end' on most of his assignments. The memory hoarding, I'm sure, came from Daddy, Grandma Florence, and of course, my Uncle Leon.

Leon Gantt had a different temperament from his brother, Robert. He was the storyteller of the family; I believe he had a gift and his memory was truly amazing. He was not as gentle as his brother Robert in temperament. In fact, he could be downright contrary, but he was an honest man and read his Bible daily. My family survived the Great Depression and two World Wars. I have many old pictures that once belonged to Uncle Leon and memorabilia from his service in North Africa and Italy. He was my main inspiration for the writing I have done. He was an extraordinary storyteller and shared his life with my siblings and me. Always willing to talk, he shared stories from his early school years, the Depression when he made gallons of moonshine, and his experiences in WWII. He was drafted into service at the age of thirty-two, considered an old man by the younger soldiers he served with, most were eighteen to twenty-two.

Uncle Leon's stories enabled me to write *Where Memories Live* and *The Return Home*. I began writing down my personal childhood memories in *The Southern Child*. This book will be a continuation of my memories, a second memoir that begins after my Daddy remarried. We are now a family of eleven, Momma Jeanette, Daddy, Grandma Florence and eight kids.

Raised in the deep South, in the quiet of the night, I remember whispers of cool breezes, the scent of sweet roses, full moons when we hurried from room to room to admire the outside sounds, crickets and night birds and the bright light shining from the heavens. There were no outside lights to interfere, we could distinguish every bush and tree the yard held, including the gleaming white sand of the driveway. The magnificence of thunderstorms and lightning strikes, when we sat quietly in the living room until the storm passed over. Sister Linda had been shocked on more than one occasion and was afraid of thunderclaps and flashes of lightening.

We all supported her with our quiet presence. There was also the love my daddy had for my stepmother, Jeanette. They married in 1962. With Momma Jeanette's four children, we became a large family in a short amount of time.

This is the rest of my story. A story, not of suspense, but of love and perseverance, how a large Southern family lived and grew together. Through good times and bad, we have lost loved ones along the way, but those left are still close. I felt it was time to record what I consider my story. As with my first memoir, *The Southern Child*, I admit my memories and those of my sisters and brothers may not coincide, but everyone has different memories. These are mine.

1. Beginnings

Imagine what a turn of events our family faced when my daddy remarried. They both had four children. Now I had three brothers, four sisters, and a new Momma. This was a big adjustment for any child. The good part was we already knew the new children from school and church. Big Steve and Linda were the same age, almost literally, their birthdays one day a part. Donnie and I were in the same grade, he was six months older than me. Lula Mae and Willette were also classmates. The classes were small at our school. One campus for grades one through twelve. You could definitely say we knew each other. The odd couple in our family was Louise, at fifteen, a full-fledged teenager, and little Steve at six, a first grader. He was the baby.

That summer of 1962, we spent almost every day together, on weekends anyway. Daddy had work during the week, on the evening shift, now at General Electric, and Momma worked at Southeastern Hatcheries in Leesville. She did not drive, so she rode to work with Mrs. Clara from church. Momma Jeanette and her children lived in a mobile home at Fairview beside her parents, Frank and Maggie Gantt. Momma Jeanette and Daddy had known each other all their lives, but there was no romantic interest between them, Daddy being eight years older. When you're a child of ten, a seventeen-year-old just sees you as a pesky kid. That span between their ages didn't matter when momma was thirty and daddy was thirty-seven. On Saturdays, daddy picked them up and we spent time together at the new house he had built. After supper, he took them home. We would see them again on Sunday morning at church. During the week on his way to work in the afternoons, he would stop by; Momma would have a piece of pie or cake wrapped for him to take to work. She was a wonderful cook. I believe there must be some truth in the adage, "the way to a man's heart is through his stomach." Even at my age, I realized they were compatible and in love, whatever that meant. Some weekends, Daddy took the whole family on a day trip, like Edisto Gardens in Orangeburg, or the trip we took to Charleston in our mint green, 1956 Ford Fairlane. Momma Jeanette and her children had never seen the ocean. They had barely traveled out of the county, much less the state. My daddy always loved to travel, take quick trips on the spur of the moment. My brother, Big Steve, years later dropped by to tell Daddy he and his family were heading to the North Carolina mountains.

"Do you and Momma want to go with us?"

Daddy reportedly replied, "Sure, just let me get my hat."

I can readily believe this, knowing his thirst for travel. Momma, on the other hand took days to pack. Still to this day, she has her suitcase out and adds clothing and necessities for a week before an actual trip. Otherwise, they were definitely well suited. Both gentle, patient and quiet Christians, wonderful parents for eight children.

Most of our weekends before their marriage were spent together playing outside. We had a couple of bikes and took turns riding them. I remember well sailing around the curve from towards Rayflin, passed the new block house, down the hill heading to the wooden house where I spent my youth. My feet were propped on the handlebars, wind blowing through my hair holding onto the back of the bicycle seat with both hands. It was like a balancing act from a circus. All of us phenomenally could do this, the bike would keep going as we pedaled as fast as we dared. Going downhill with no hands was the most thrilling part.

We also laid out a baseball diamond in the pine thicket behind the house. We first cleared the baselines by raking away the pine straw to clear a path around the bases. Pine straw can be really slippery when running from base to base. We didn't have a real baseball bat, so Big Steve, already into carpentry, made us one. It was a 1x6 inch piece of lumber with a handle cut out at one end big enough for us to hold with two hands and swing at the ball coming across the plate. We had great fun playing baseball in the pine thicket. Somehow, we usually missed the trees. It was normally boys against girls. But to be fair, one of us girls had to take one for the team and play on the boy's side. That was decided by drawing straws.

The main thing I remember about those baseball games was Big Steve standing at the wrong place at the wrong time. He stood too close to Louise when she was at bat. When she hit the ball, she didn't just drop the bat and run to first. She would sling the bat in the air behind her and high tail it to first. Steve got hit in the face, a one-inch bruise appeared almost instantly across his eyes. The edge of the 1x6 board hit him at an angle across his nose and left eye. He could have been knocked out cold or worse. He sported a purple and black shiner for weeks afterward. We soon got a real baseball bat, but with the six-inch-wide flat board it was almost impossible to miss any pitch remotely close. The regulation bat was harder. And, we all learned a lesson; don't stand too close to Louise when she was up to bat.

Country kids of the 60's could invent entertainment. With

only three television channels, we sometimes came up with some crazy games. I remember one dark night that first summer; the moon was full, giving us enough light to play outside. We had a bucket and searched the yard front and back collecting every toad frog in the vicinity. Why? Just something to do. It was easy around the porches where the little toads hung out waiting for insects drawn to the ceiling lights. We had half a bucket full in no time. I don't think Louise, Lula Mae, or Willette participated, they were tooooo grown up for such silliness. The rest of us were game, even though we had been told by the grown-ups, "If a frog pees on you, you'll get warts"

Uncle Leon had some secret wisdom as to how to remove warts. I knew this to be true, he had actually removed a wart off the inside of my right index finger, not with his pocket knife or any type of medicine. He just rubbed it and said that it would go away and two weeks later it had disappeared.

Back to the frogs, we had fun running around outside in the dark and scooping up the toads. We counted them all and freed them, then retreated inside. I can't remember the number in the bucket, but it was a lot. Now I wouldn't even touch a nasty little toad, guess I got grown up too.

Another fun game we came up with that first summer was riding pine saplings. A couple of us would push the sapling over at the trunk until one of the boys could grab the top branches and pulling the sapling until the top almost touched the ground. The pine was maybe ten feet tall, so the trunk was flexible and was easily pushed over. When it touched the ground, one of the others would climb on board while another acted as an anchor keeping the top near the ground. I envisioned a rodeo bronco rider and when it was my turn, I realized immediately there would be no staying on for eight seconds. Holding on really tight was a must.

The anchor would release the sapling and the sapling whirled upward in a futile attempt to return to the upright position. When the sapling stilled, we would release our grip, jump backward and tumble on the ground. It was really a fun ride. That consumed most of one afternoon and there were visually several pine saplings that were temporarily bent slightly, but no permanent damage.

It was a fun summer for all of us, Momma loved to cook, so did Grandma. They seemed to get along fine. Grandma took well to the prospect of a larger family. I only heard her say one negative comment. She said, "I don't understand why Robert wants to marry a woman with so many children."

Pretty soon she became close to Little Steve. He would sit on the arm of her chair and comb her hair. She seemed to enjoy that. She was seventy-five when they married. Robert being her only child, I understand she had conflicting feelings. She, of course, wanted him to be happy, but probably felt a little left out, another woman becoming number one in his affections, not his momma. Momma Jeanette was kind to her and tolerant, so there were no major disruptions or hurt feelings.

When we all sat around the table for a meal, Big Steve, always the comedian, would tease Grandma. Little Steve would giggle through the whole meal at everything he said. I could tell she did not take well to his teasing. Once she asked him to put rice on her outstretched plate. "I only want a few grains please." Of course, being the comedian in the family, he took her request literally and put three grains on her plate.

She was not pleased. "I wanted more than that," she replied in a huff.

"Well Grandma," he stated with a straight face, "I was just doing what you asked." Of course, Little Steve was busy covering his mouth, trying not to break out in peals of laughter.

Grandma was raised very poor, but with a strong Christian influence and manners. Whenever she finished with a meal, she always said, "I need to be excused." We would sometimes giggle when she said that, 'beexcued' came out as one word. She also said that when she needed to go to the bathroom, so of course we found that expression funny.

Mealtime was always like this, the comedian, Big Steve, just trying to entertain and insert humor into our Norman Rockwell ritual. All eleven of us, crowded around one table, bowing our heads and my daddy saying grace. We were a bit old for the make pretty hands part. Otherwise, it was the same, palms together and bowed heads.

Poor Grandma was usually the target of Steve's entertaining attempts. She never could quiet pronounce spaghetti; it always came out 'begetti.' After all, when Grandma was a child growing up in the country, in a sharecropper family, they had no idea what Italian food was. It was mostly biscuits, milk gravy, fried fatback, and fried chicken on Sundays. But her family gathered around the table as a unit. Their clothes much simpler, overalls and house dresses, simple fare, but blessing the food was a must.

* * *

There was a hole dug, about two feet deep by three feet long, in the backyard slanted downward. This was where we burned the trash, paper or cardboard. No trash pick-up in those days or recycle centers to take discarded items, especially on back roads in the country. Recycling was not even a thought. Broken dishes, cans, and anything that would not burn was hauled to the trash pile, way up in the woods above the old house.

One day Grandma disappeared and we began to look for her.

I observed from the kitchen window the two Steves standing around that hole. When investigating, I saw Grandma's tousled gray head peeping above the edge. As I approached, Big Steve was looking down seriously asking, "Grandma, what are you doing down there?"

Grandma red faced, replied, "I slipped in and I couldn't get out."

The two helped her stand up and walk up the slanted incline. Grandma was fine, nothing broken. And again, Big Steve got his laugh, though not from Grandma.

* * *

Daddy and Momma set their wedding date as August 11, 1962. They were married at the Reverend and Mrs. Richard Abel's home on Convent Church Road. Mrs. Abel made a wedding cake and had a small reception in their dining room for the couple.

They were married in the pastor's living room. All of us children, along with Grandma, sat on their sofa. Louise was the only child absent; she was away at FHA (Future Homemakers of America) camp. So, the story of all of us together begins. Momma Jeanette and Daddy went to North Carolina on their honeymoon, leaving Grandma Florence, age seventy-five, in charge of all eight of us. That, of course, was a joke; she was just a chaperone. We had all been raised by God fearing parents, with manners and respect for our elders, so when they returned after two nights away, the house was still standing.

There were a lot of changes to be made. In the beginning, there were two double beds in the girls' room, Louise, Willette and Lula Mae slept in one. Linda and I slept in the other. Donnie and Little Steve slept in Big Steve's small bedroom next to the bathroom and Big Steve slept in a twin bed in the room with

Grandma. Momma and Daddy had their own room to the right of the living room.

A big priority became an addition to the house. We also would need a bigger car, a station wagon, something besides a 1956 Ford Fairlane. All these hurdles would be breeched in good time. Kids are so resilient and we would have all been happy sleeping on the floor on pallets. The very first thing we had to contend with, only two weeks after the wedding, was school.

2. School Begins

Only two weeks after the consolidation of our families, all eight of us had to start another year of school at Pelion. We had all been going to the same school together for years and the bus driver, I believe one of the Shumpert boys, either Douglas or Henry, stopped and picked us up. After we got to school, there was no big registration process; we just went to class for that grade. Pelion was a very small school and there was only one class for each grade 1st through 6th making it extremely easy for the registration process. Books were all rented and book covers we made from brown paper grocery bags. We may have paid 10- or 12-dollars total cost to rent our books. There was no list of school supplies to buy. Paper and pencils were the standard requirements. No fancy book bags, we didn't use those. Boys usually had a clamp board; girls would use a three-ring binder for our notebook paper and books were stacked on top. Depending on the grade, a couple of spiral notebooks might be needed, especially for grades seven through twelve. Students in those grades had different teachers for different subjects, so we had to move from one class to another. We went to Kmart after we had started school if more than paper and pencils were required.

Every classroom had a fancy pencil sharpener. At least we

thought it deserved that designation, attached to one of the outside window sills, sometimes we stood in line in order to get our pencils trimmed. We very seldom used ink pens, except for term papers or special assignments. Classrooms were heated with radiators on the outside wall. When the temperature outside began to rise in the Spring, pushing up the windows was our only option. Sometimes a wayward insect would fly into the room and assault the students. Flies were the most prevalent. I don't remember anyone ever getting a bee sting with the windows up in any classes. All the pupils were pretty much country kids. We were conditioned to ignore insects, even stinging ones; they were so much a part of our outside life. That was where we spent most of our time. We did have screens on the windows at home, but paid insects no attention. Any flying insect that made it inside, we dispatched with a fly swatter. Crawling insects were stepped on. Air conditioning was just now beginning to revolutionize the South, but not yet at Pelion School.

* * *

Next to Mrs. Snelgrove's room in the auditorium building was the sick room, with two beds. Mrs. Snelgrove was in charge of nursing duties. Depending on the injury or the complaint, she decided if it was necessary to send a student home. Otherwise, she took their temperature. Depending on the reading, the patient was given aspirin and directed to lay down in one of the two beds to rest. An hour later, their temperature was retaken and they were assessed accordingly. Higher, the parent was contacted to pick their child up; temperature gone, back to class. Thinking back, at this point, there was not yet phone service in the country where I lived. I guess, if the student needed to go home, someone was designated to take them. If there was an injury such as skinned elbows or knees, any bleeding was stopped with compression, then iodine and a bandage. Students were, of course, sent home if there was nausea, vomiting, or anything worse, like a fall that could mean a broken bone. I spent some time resting in one of those beds, and to be honest, it was usually because I was tired. Frequently, students just got bored in the sick room, cracked the door to her classroom, and said, "Mrs. Snelgrove, I feel much better, can I go back to class?"

* * *

When school started, so soon after Momma and Daddy were married, that had to be the first priority. To Kmart we went to pick up all necessary items, including articles of clothing. All us girls had to have dresses or skirts and blouses, no shorts, jeans or long pants allowed. The boys had to have long pants too, but they may have been allowed to wear jeans, dungarees, or even denim overalls. Pelion was, after all, a farming community. I know the girls usually had to have one or two dresses. With the difference in ages, anything too small, could be passed down.

We signed up for band, glee club, basketball etc. I was never a sports person, more into reading and writing. I did, however, hate to diagram sentences. History and reading were my favorite subjects. Reading was a euphemism for literature class, at least in high school. We had books assigned to read and, oh joy, give a book report in front of the class. As a high school junior, I did write a term paper exploring the poetry of Emily Dickinson. Otherwise, real literature would wait until I took college courses.

I signed up for band my first year after Daddy and Momma married. I played the clarinet. Played is not the right word. I never practiced. But was in the marching band. I think more bodies were needed, not talent. I chose the clarinet because it was in a small case, which had to be lugged home from school every day in order to practice. The practice part was my downfall. I never did much of that. We all signed up for band that year, except for Little Steve. He was too young. Louise played the French horn, Willette played the baritone, and Big Steve played the trombone. I do know Donnie took band, but I am not sure which instrument. My sister, Lula Mae, just recently told me she signed up for the trombone, but quit after the first day, that trombone case was probably too big to lug around. The cost of band was only $10 a year, which included the rental of the instrument. I believe only Louise and Willette were really serious about practicing their musical instruments. I guess that was why they, along with myself, climbed up on the roof of the house one evening, standing on the peak, we three played Taps as the sun was setting over the river swamp. I could play that. Otherwise, those two, Louise and Willette, were the only serious musicians.

Even at the yearly fee of only $10, that was hard for Daddy and Momma to pay along with our book rent and our lunch money. Lunch cost was one dollar a week which included a glass bottle of milk. All these monies were collected in home room and turned into the office in grades one through six. Once a student reached seventh grade, the homeroom teacher was responsible for passing out her class books and collecting lunch money. Beginning in seventh grade we received a lunch ticket, a different color for each week. The cost was still the same, $1.00 a week and remained so until I graduated. Daddy started the job with General Electric, making more money than in a cotton mill, but still barely enough for a large family. We struggled through.

Pelion School had three main buildings: The Grammar School

Building, the auditorium and a middle building containing the Library, Lunchroom and Band room.

The Grammar School building was two-story brick with a one-story main office attached to the front. Stepping out of the office in this building, on either side were classrooms that were utilized for upper classmen, otherwise all the classrooms in this building were for grammar school children.

The auditorium building had a stage at one end and the basketball court. The nets and back boards were on either end. Of course, that meant the floor, by necessity, had painted lines and circles as all basketball courts do. This floor was wooden and had to be kept waxed and shiny. The back boards folded up during plays, contests or any stage performance. The thick red velvet curtains were closed during games and students frequently sat on the edge of the stage to watch. The bleachers were four high, stationary and built as wide steps. Entering the auditorium building through the main entrance, free standing bookshelves were in the foyer. These shelves were used by students to stack their books when attending one of the two classes in this building. Past the foyer to the left was Mrs. Snelgrove's classroom, lots of typewriters on desks. At the end of the hall was the sickroom, behind that and only accessible from her classroom was the mimeograph room where the school newspaper, the Sandspur, was printed.

To the right in the main hall was the entrance to Mrs. Robinson's high school English class. The desks in both these classrooms were sturdily built oak desks with a detached oak chair. There was an indentation at the top of each desk specifically designed for a pencil or pen, hopefully to assure they would stay put. There was also a cubby underneath the top of the desk large enough for a book or two and a notebook. Mrs. Snelgrove taught business classes and sponsored the FBLA (Future Business Leaders of America).

Typing, Shorthand, and Bookkeeping were her specialties, and of course, supervising sick students.

From the hallway there were two sets of double doors with windows in the top section. These doors accessed the auditorium itself and were kept closed, except for ballgames or stage productions.

During recess, we were, however, allowed to enter the auditorium to use the vending machines in a room to the right of the stage on level with the gym floor. This room had a cement floor. We had to be particular about walking across the gym, didn't want to scuff the shiny finish, no running allowed. There were two drink machines and a snack machine that held packs of peanuts, candy bars, and cookies. A dime would buy a glass bottle of Coca Cola, Pepsi, Nehi orange, RC Cola, or Tab. The snack machine was only a nickel. Put in a nickel or dime and pull the round button handle underneath what you wanted and your selection would drop down into a metal tray. There also were double doors that exited this room to the outside.

The other main building contained the library presided over by Mrs. Nichols, the Home Economics complex. I would consider it that because it had a closet lined with shelves, three separate kitchens (no walls between), a row of sewing machines, and tables and chairs. There was also what I considered a secret room, an opening, no door, on the far wall where there was a sofa, a couple of chairs, and an ironing board tucked away for pressing our sewing. This library wing also housed the science room, with jars of disgusting things preserved in formaldehyde. In my Biology class, I had the distinct pleasure of dissecting a frog, which convinced me I was not destined for the medical field.

Every Life Tells a Story

* * *

The most important part of this center building besides Library, Science room, and Home Economics department, was the lunchroom in the middle. Entering the door, to the left was a large kitchen counter where students picked up their trays and slid them on the extended metal bar and told the cafeteria personnel what they wanted. Of course, there was a meat and two vegetables usually available, so no real choice. Only if you didn't want one of these. We also had a dessert, peach or cherry cobbler, sometime ice cream cup or just plain canned sliced peaches or pears. The one good thing about being out of grammar school, you could sit with your friends, not with a teacher. The teachers all sat together at the last row of tables near the exit to the rear. They even had to pay more a week for their lunch, $1.25. When we finished with our lunch, we took our trays, hard green plastic reusable, sectioned plates, scraped out any excess food in a big pan, and deposited the trays, plates, and utensils in an open window. I believe all these had to be washed by hand in a big sink with lots of hot, soapy water. There was no electric dishwasher to clean and sanitize these plates, this was in the early 1960's.

To the right of the lunchroom entrance, under a covered porch, was the entrance to the Band Room, Mr. Helm's domain. It was a large room where band practice took place. Across a narrow hall from the practice area was the small room where instruments were stored.

Past the Band Department was the shop, where all manner of saws, hammers, woodworking tools, mechanical instruments, wrenches, screw drivers, anything needed to repair motors or tools for woodworking could be found. I do not remember ever going into the shop area. Boys took shop and were members of the FFA

(Future Farmers of America) and they had a classroom somewhere in the shop department. At that time, girls did not take shop or go to trade school. There was a bus that took boys to trade school one day a week, they had a special bus driver. I have not a clue where trade school was at that time.

Later, at the back of this Band/Shop building there were two classrooms and a guidance office. Miss Powell taught an English class in one room, the same room still held the chest freezer in front of the back windows where we bought ice cream from Mr. Crouch, the Janitor, at recess. The other room was where Mr. Stover taught Agriculture and the FFA met. During my early grammar school years, these rooms contained all manner of equipment for canning, I never knew if it was for local produce, but I do remember looking past Mr. Crouch while ordering my ice cream and seeing equipment and conveyor belts.

3. Seventh Grade

I can remember the first day of seventh grade as if it were yesterday. Probably because I now considered myself a high school student, really junior high, but I didn't have to sit in one classroom all day. I remember sitting on the bus close to the front with my friend, Nancy. We were so excited about the new year.

I had on a dress the color of a feverish child's cheek. It was pink, very pink, and there was a cloth covered belt of the same shade. There was no decoration on this dress, just v neck with two or three pink buttons and a flared skirt.

As we entered the outskirts of the small community of Pelion on highway 178, we passed the Smith's house on the left and Mrs. Dorn's gray stone house on the right, Mrs. Dorn taught at Pelion, but was never my teacher. Her daughter, Donette, was in my class in high school. Coming into Pelion, the bus made a sharp turn to the right between the St. John's Lutheran Church and the home of Mrs. Blanche Gantt.

I had already had my required 'new school year' perm. Momma took us to Miss Hazel. She had a small block beauty shop next to her house at Fairview crossroads and was our local hair style consultant. As you can imagine, my short hair was quite curly and had that new perm smell, which lingered for about a week. I recall it was an iron-clad rule back then, no shampooing your newly permed hair for at least five days.

***

Seventh grade was a memorable year for me and my classmates. We all felt like we were really high school students, no longer stuck in grammar school. Miss Ruth Gunter was my homeroom teacher. She and her sister Miss Doris, who taught me Home Economics, were both single, never married. Miss Ruth was a super sweet lady, completely white-haired. She did teach at Fairview High School, where my daddy graduated in 1940. Miss Ruth was born in 1899 and lived to be one hundred and one. She retired from teaching shortly after she taught me in seventh grade in 1963.

I was elected as one of the class officers that year, along with William, Marion, Stanley, and Steve, the only girl, and secretary-treasurer. I have a picture of the officers, and I stand at a noticeable distance from the boys. At that age, we considered boys to be uninteresting, I guess, I didn't want to stand too close. I do remember the blue blouse and checkered culottes I was wearing. We had class meetings, don't remember how often, but I do still have the blue spiral notebook I used to take minutes. Why did I keep it, I don't know, I keep the strangest things? I do recall collecting money from class members to buy Miss Ruth an end of year present. She taught me English and Reading. I'm certain of this, because I have all my report cards, first grade through twelfth. I earned a B+ in both for the year. Back then, a B+ was 90-94. I started to say, Miss Ruth gave me a B+ for the final grade, but actually I earned it.

During seventh and eighth grades, students who had a high-grade average after the third six weeks and the sixth six weeks could exempt the semester exams. I don't know what that average was, but in seventh grade I exempted all exams, except for band. No surprise there! In eighth grade I wasn't required to take any exams. I really thought I was a genius, more like a smarty pants. I was the only student in my class to exempt Mrs. O'Daniel's science exams. After eighth grade, that stopped. I quickly became humble again about my intelligence. I made a D on Mrs. Robinson's English exam in ninth grade. I reread the whole eleven chapters for Mrs. Snelgrove's bookkeeping/office practice exam in eleventh grade and earned a big fat F on that exam. Taught myself a valuable lesson, everyone has the same potential, it's all in how you use it and don't abuse it.

Back to the seventh grade, Billy Gene Stone, my favorite teacher, taught History. He also, for some unknown reason, had me enter a speech contest for Lexington School District 1. Maybe, I was a big talker in his class too. That, of course, had nothing to do with giving a speech in front of judges. There was also a student from 8th grade, Ann Laird, who participated in the contest. I don't remember anything about the speech. Mr. Stone took Ann and me to Lexington for the contest. I totally bombed, along with Ann. I do remember Mr. Stone took me home that night, after stopping in Pelion to pick up his father to ride with us. I believe that was to make me feel more comfortable. Maybe, he didn't feel too keen about driving by himself on those lonely, dark, dirt roads, no phones, and sparsely settled without any security lights along the way. In today's political climate, he would also be protecting himself. I have a newspaper clipping in my scrapbook of the participants in the speaking event. Some things are just too important to throw away.

Previously I mentioned reading class as a euphemism for literature, that I had to wait until college classes to actually study literature. The exception was my term paper I did on that great poet, Emily Dickerson, for eleventh grade English. That would have been Mrs. Robinson's class. She was tough and had the disposition of someone who expected every instruction to be obeyed, never ignored. I still have that term paper, including a pencil drawing of Miss Dickerson. I earned an A, dated September 22, 1967. She was a tough but fair teacher and I was very pleased with my grade.

4. More Room

The next important requirement at home: we had to have more space. Daddy had to work and we needed more space right away. He and Uncle Leon started on the addition, two bedrooms on the end of the house. Daddy could only work mornings and on weekends because he worked second shift at the General Electric plant near Lexington. One of those bedrooms was for Louise, Lula Mae, and Willette, the other for the three boys, Donnie, Big Steve, and Little Steve.

When we moved into the new house, the kitchen cabinets were just a skeleton, no doors or finished counter tops. The cabinets in the kitchen had been finished and plumbing completed, so all that was needed was the extra bedrooms. From the front porch, you entered the living room, to the right was Momma Jeanette and Daddy's room, a door led from the living room into the heating hall where a fuel oil heater was ready to provide heat. Beside the heater was the door to the only bathroom. Grandma's rocker was squeezed in between the heater and a white metal table which would later hold our telephone. We got a telephone in the mid 60's and it was a party line.

We would soon become notorious for being late for church and all other events. The clock on the wall above the kitchen stove was even set up twenty minutes fast, which made no difference whatsoever, we were well aware the time was incorrect. It did not help with the tardiness. The biggest obstacle I'm sure was the one bathroom, for five girls.

The kitchen was in the back-right corner, with a door leading outside to the unfinished back porch. It was just lined with blocks, the cement floor had to be poured. The tile on the kitchen floor was large green and yellow squares, glue spread on the floor in a thin layer with a notched trowel and the rubber tiles carefully placed. The table and chairs were retro 50's yellow top with metal around the sides and yellow vinyl padded-back chairs with metal legs. The refrigerator, the first year we lived there was the old kind, no shelves on the inside door, small freezer at the top with metal ice cube trays. This refrigerator had to be defrosted which was a very undesirable chore and of course it had very little space for frozen food.

Momma and Daddy always went to Winn Dixie in Batesburg and bought groceries for the week. The grocery receipt looked about three feet long and they usually spent about eighty dollars, which was exorbitantly high for the early 1960's. They didn't buy junk food. Momma always cooked the meals, vegetables and meat, she was always experimenting with new recipes. Every week they brought home one bag of candy. One of the boys would immediately open it and dispense it into eight piles. Of course, the rest of us had to watch to make sure it was divided correctly and the sibling knew how to count. They also bought a few Coca Colas. These we hoarded to add to our sweet tea at mealtimes, half sweet tea, half coke. It was very good and we all got to share the Cokes.

Eventually, we got a much bigger refrigerator and even a chest freezer that sat against the wall, right before exiting to the heating hall.

The heating hall on the other end had three exit doors, one to Steve's original small bedroom, which became a junk room, filled with boxes of Grandma's quilting scraps, treadle sewing machine, and pie safe my Granddaddy Kelly built in 1930, two others to the bedrooms. On the right side, the first bedroom was Grandma's and another door led from her room into the boys' room. There was a double bed and a twin bed in their room with chest of drawers and a small closet. Also, an outside exit door with a very small covered porch.

The door to the left exiting the heating hall led to the girls' wing. I slept in the first room on a double bed with Linda, there was also a dresser with mirror, small closet, and a sofa that had belonged to Momma Jeanette. Through our room was Lula Mae, Willette, and Louise's room. It also contained a double bed and a twin bed. Louise, as the eldest, got the bed to herself. They had chest of drawers, dresser with mirror, and a sizeable closet for hanging dresses, blouses, and skirts. We had very few long pants and no jeans that I can remember. We did own shorts for summer, but these articles of clothing were not allowed in school. There was a pass-through door from the girls' room into the boys, it had a latch on the girl's side. I guess it was a safety precaution, in case of fire the closest exit door was from the boys' room, an outside door, top half with glass panes and a very small covered porch. As you can imagine, the connecting door between the girl's rooms was always locked, no boys allowed in our side.

5. Christmas 1962

Our first Christmas as a family was in 1962. I remember well that Christmas, we still searched the woods for a Christmas tree, just like when we were living in the old house. Except this year there were eight of us. It was still a thrill to find just the right tree and we spent a lot of time searching the woods around the old house and down near the swamp.

We found the cedar we were looking for a couple of weeks before Christmas. I ran down a leaf covered hill to a small gully at the edge of the swamp, tripped over a broken pine limb and went sprawling in a heap at the bottom. My ankle was badly sprained and I couldn't put my weight on it. Of course, the others thought I was just faking and threatened to leave me to hop home on one foot. After begging and pleading, they all finally agreed to take turns helping me hop home. I could hop on the good leg with support by wrapping my arm around someone on either side to keep me upright. It was probably a half mile to the house and you can imagine how much grumbling and complaining I had to hear all the way home. It was slow going, hopping on one foot, but we finally got there.

The next day, Momma Jeanette let me stay home from school. I definitely couldn't walk and the side of my right foot and ankle were badly swollen and purple. I hope they felt some remorse for all their complaining and whining. I doubt it. At least they knew I was not faking the injury, since Momma told me to stay home.

* * *

Christmas Eve. Momma and Daddy had concocted some lame story about having to go to Batesburg. They left all eight of us with Aunt Fannie and Uncle Willie, who still were living in the Steadman House out on the highway. Little Steve was only in the first grade and they didn't want to destroy the magic of Santa bringing toys for him. The rest of us were wise to their trick.

It was winter and cold that Christmas. The huge old house Aunt Fannie and Uncle Willie lived in had no heat but wood. We had to all huddle around the blazing fire in the kitchen. Their kitchen had high ceilings and of course no insulation, so we sat around close to the fireplace.

Uncle Willie and Aunt Fannie were glad to have all us kids and Grandma there for a few hours. Uncle Willie was in his element with his wad of tobacco in his cheek, spit can on the floor, dressed in overalls, long sleeved shirt underneath, and a stocking cap on his bald head. I can close my eyes and see him now in that red knit cap chewing his tobacco. He loved to tell ghost stories and about the ghosts that haunted their old mansion. All of us kids loved his stories. I wish I could remember them. They usually included graveyards, strange lights and balls of fire floating in the air. I do recollect one story about an attractive young woman wearing high heels that he sometimes heard and saw entering their bedroom in the mornings. He would talk a while, pause to spit the tobacco juice in his can, then continue with the story. I think Little Steve was especially enthralled.

Momma and Daddy finally returned from their supposed errand to town and we went home. Surprise! Santa had come to our house while we were gone. Santa's gifts were not wrapped. For some reason, I don't know why, I asked for a basketball with back board and hoop. Well, I got it. Daddy put it up on one of the pine trees in the thicket behind the house and the boys really appreciated it.

After that Christmas, Santa no longer delivered presents in his sleigh. The magic had disappeared for all of us, including Little Steve. He found out Santa was not a real person. After that Christmas, we still did the tree search and Daddy set it up in the stand for us to decorate, but we were grown up, or thought we were. Daddy and Momma would go shopping and close their bedroom door and wrap presents together. They did this almost every night two weeks before Christmas. This year, they had a brand-new idea. They didn't put our names on the presents, they made up a code with letters, so we didn't know what gifts belonged to who. The code on mine was LL, the first letter of my name was K, so they used two L's, the next letter in the alphabet. The two Steves became LTT for Little Steve and BTT for Big Steve. Willette was XX and Donnie was EE. Louise was BMM, since she was bigger and Lula Mae was LMM. They thought it was ingenious, we thought it stunk and were really mad. We did not hesitate to express our displeasure at their bright idea, respectfully of course. They never did that again.

6. On the Road Again

We finally got a bigger car. The 1956 Ford was just not large enough for the whole family to travel in comfort. Daddy traded in the '56 for a 1963 gold Rambler station wagon. It was a small wagon, but did have three seats. The third seat faced backward and had to be entered and exited by the back door, basically those in this seat had to have the door opened for them from the outside. It swung open wide and was not really convenient. The boys usually sat in this third seat and were not happy.

After about six months, Daddy got rid of the Rambler and bought a 1963 Ford Galaxy station wagon. It was white, also had three seats, all facing forward and had much more room. The boys were still relegated to the third seat, but they could unlatch one of the second seats, fold it down and climb in. There was space behind the third seat for luggage and the tail gate folded down for easy excess. We were all happy with the Ford station wagon. Daddy, Momma, and Grandma occupied the front, we five girls sat in the second seat and the boys were in the third. There was no seat belt law at that time, besides the station wagon had no seatbelts. And, of course, no air conditioning.

I have some good memories associated with that white station wagon, maybe not all good, but memorable associations anyway.

Once, after Louise got her drivers' licenses, probably in 1964, Daddy, Lula Mae, Louise, and I were driving down to the old house to do some work in the garden. I don't remember all the particulars, but Louise was driving, I was in the front seat with her. Lula Mae and Daddy were sitting on the folded down tailgate. There were some gardening tools in the back. It was a short drive, probably two hundred yards to the garden down the slope behind the old house. All started out fine, beautiful sunny day in late spring, windows were rolled down to let in the cooling breeze. The problem started when a bee flew in the window and begin harassing Louise, the driver. Instead of staying calm, she decided we needed to kill that bee. Reaching down with one hand, Louise slipped off her flip flop. The bee was buzzing around inside the windshield when she decided to strike. That's when things went terribly wrong. Concentrating more on the bee than the road, she veered into the ditch beside the road. This was, still is, a dirt road and so it was more than just a little dip. The tailgate folded up with Daddy and Lula Mae. They were thrown into the back among the gardening tools. By the time Daddy and Lula Mae untangled themselves from the surprise fold up in the back and climbed out, our Daddy already had a black and purple shiner. He was not in a good mood! The maddest I ever saw him, but to our surprise he more or less seethed in silence, except for a few brief exasperated questions to Louise.

"What in the world were you doing?"

"Were you not paying attention?" Daddy asked in a heated tone.

Louise didn't say much and the exchange did not last long, but to our surprise, Daddy didn't use the first curse word. He never did that anyway, but this would have been the appropriate time, if ever. Things soon cooled down; the garden visit was cancelled so my Daddy could put an ice pack on his eye. We never knew what he hit his eye on, we could only suspect, maybe the corner of the seat. It really looked bad for a couple of weeks and I'm sure he took some teasing at work. but we all laughed about it later, even Daddy. Much later, of course, as in years.

* * *

That would not be the last time my Daddy's patience would be tested when one of us drove that white station wagon.

When I turned fourteen, my Daddy took me to Batesburg to take my written test for my driver's permit. I passed and was all excited about getting a drivers' licenses, but definitely not right away.

On the way home from Batesburg, Daddy stopped the car on the long stretch of dirt road between Steadman and home. The road was, of course, dirt and bumpy as a scrub board.

"You drive the rest of the way home," Daddy said.

"Are you sure, Daddy, I have never driven before?"

"It's not far, may as well start practicing."

Daddy opened the door, came around the car, and I slid over behind the wheel.

"Just take it slow, you'll be fine."

I wasn't as confident. I was especially leery of crossing the pond damn, but all went well. I didn't meet any other cars, thank God. When I got to the turn-in to our front yard, I was going a little too fast and I didn't turn at the right time.

"I'll just turn here," I remember saying. There was another drive on the far side.

I turned in and faced a good-sized pine tree; it just appeared out of nowhere and I was headed straight for it.

Daddy was shouting, "Put on the brakes, put on the brakes!"

Well, I didn't and we slammed into the pine. In my defense, I wasn't even sure where the brake pedal was, I had not had any training what-so-ever.

Daddy said, "It's my fault, I thought you knew more about driving then you did."

He had the bumper repaired and light replaced and never mentioned the incident again. Of course, I didn't get off that easy with my brothers and sisters.

7. Vacation Time

With a family as large as ours, we had to make adjustments and learn to give and take.

When school closed for summer vacation, Daddy always planned a trip. He loved to go to the mountains of North Carolina and Tennessee. A favorite spot was The Great Smoky Mountains national park. We went every summer on a short mountain vacation. We had the most fun when we were all together, before graduations, weddings, and college intruded. As a family we would traipse off to the mountains for a few days.

Once, we actually went to Ruby Falls, south of Chattanooga, Tennessee, below Lookout Mountain, by below I mean, under Lookout Mountain. I believe summer of 1963. There are pictures of us in pairs sitting under a stone arch with a sign Welcome to Ruby Falls over our heads. My picture was with Donnie.

I was not personally thrilled with Ruby Falls. We got on an elevator at the top of Lookout Mountain and went straight down about three hundred feet. The doors opened and a guide led the group along an underground pathway, through magnificent rock formations with appropriate subdued lighting tucked behind curtains of stone. There were stalagmites and stalactites all along the trail. Water containing calcium dripped from the roof to form mineral build up on the cave floor. The icicle-shaped formations hanging from the roof (stalactites) dripped calcium infused drops of water to the floor to form candle shaped columns of stone (stalagmites). The process of forming these stone shapes took millions of years. Our guide explained this process and the how and when the cave and waterfall was discovered. All I could think about was all the mine cave-ins we had seen on television, and the possibility of being covered under tons of rock.

Our guide commented with a smile, "If we have a cave-in, you can't be buried deeper, any cheaper."

That statement was not at all amusing to me and did not ease my concern in the least. I was ready to go to the surface right then and there. Following our guide, we came to the end of the dark underground trail, before me I saw a beautiful waterfall pouring from an undefinable aperture in the roof over three hundred feet to a pool below. Various colors: green, red, yellow, and blue lights began to play off the falling water. This was Ruby Falls named after the wife of the man who actually discovered it in 1928. I was beginning to think it was well worth the trip underground, but there was one more treat.

"Everyone, please stay perfectly still, we are going to turn off all the lights, just so you can experience total darkness," our guide informed us.

I did not need to experience absolute absence of light three hundred feet below ground. But we were not asked beforehand. It was so dark I had a hard time locating the nose on my face. The darkness didn't last more than sixty seconds, just enough time for our pupils to adjust to the black all around. Surprisingly, we all endured it in silence. If it had been more than that brief time, I'm sure we would have all started screaming, "Turn on the lights!" That was the climax of the cave visit and I believe every single person in our group had enjoyed as much as they could stand. The guide led us back along the narrow trail to the elevator and there was an audible sigh of relief as we started to move upward to the surface. Once out in the open air and sunshine, I fleetingly thought about dropping to my knees and kissing the ground. Just kidding, but that was my one and only trip to see the waterfall in the cave.

* * *

All eight of us kids plus Daddy, Momma, and Grandma went, probably summer of 1964, to visit the mountains of North Carolina and Tennessee. We were headed this time to The Great Smoky Mountains National Park. It was the best. We were so excited. We had discussed, weeks before the trip, what a beautiful place it was and what fun we would have, visiting souvenir shops, wading in the river, and taking in the majesty of the tall mountain peaks covered with trees. Traveling curvy mountain roads, ears popping from the change in altitude, and actually drive among the wispy white clouds.

We had packed the car the night before with shared suitcases containing our clothes, and food items that did not need to be kept cold, loaves of bread, jars of mayo, our favorite cookies, chips, and snacks. The cold drinks, Momma's homemade pimento cheese, boloney, pickle loaf, dip for the chips, potato salad, and a couple bars of cream cheese were ready to go to be placed in the Coleman cooler with all the ice trays emptied on top early the next morning.

Departure time was set at no later than 4 A.M. No problem getting us up that early. This was going to be a grand adventure for us all, and my Daddy was a big believer in vacations, even short ones. We piled into the car, pitch dark outside, long before daylight.

Suitcases, cooler, and food were behind the third seat where the boys were sitting.

There was no interstate highway system yet, and we had to travel to the up country on back roads through towns like Greenwood, Belton, Honea Path, Ware Shoals, Greenville, Travellers Rest, and Anderson. We were all too excited to nap. Just as the sun begin to turn night into gray dawn, we were in the foothills of South Carolina's Blue Ridge mountains. The paved mountain roads began to weave in and out and among the low tree-covered hills, getting higher as we traveled northwest toward North Carolina. We were oohing and aahing about the mountains and the scenery on all sides. Before we crossed the state line, Daddy pointed out the Welcome to North Carolina sign.

It was a bright sunny day as we crossed into North Carolina headed for Cherokee. Back then Cherokee was mostly a tourist destination: lots of souvenir shops, an authentic Indian village to visit, and Indian warriors dressed in traditional garb with long feathered head dresses. These elaborately dressed Indians offered photographs with tourists for a fee. With their fancy headdresses, leather fringed shirts and pants with beadwork, they must have all been portraying tribal chiefs. They, of course, were friendly fellows and didn't mind a conversation. I did notice they all had southern accents, I guess because they were Southern Cherokees. There were no casinos to gamble in or street signs with the additional Cherokee language names added. We were headed for Craig's Motor Court. We had a reservation for a house called a bungalow there, three bedrooms, a kitchen, dining area, and two bathrooms. My Daddy had to write a letter to make our reservation, no phone at home yet.

We unloaded all our suitcases and headed for the National Park and the entrance outside Cherokee on the North Carolina side. Driving through the park, there were campgrounds and side trips to Cade's Cove and lots of overlooks for picture opportunities. Daddy always took lots of pictures. This was many years before digital cameras, our camera was a brownie with a flash bulb. Daddy always sent the rolls of film to Jack Rabbit in Spartanburg to be developed. This took some time, that's why, I have pictures taken at a Christmas parade with an April date on the edge of the photo. Same problem with vacation pictures, the date could be October or November, not in the summer.

Before actually entering the park, we added more ice to the cooler, draining the excess water, so we could stop for a picnic at one of the many cement tables with benches along the park highway. We stopped beside the Little Pigeon River at a roadside picnic area, covered the table with a tablecloth Momma had remembered to bring, and extra towels to cover the benches. She and Daddy spread the food out while we headed down a rocky path to the river. Wading in the cold water in the swift current, stepping gingerly from slippery rock to rock was our favorite thing to do. Every time we went to the mountains, we picnicked in the park and always begged Daddy to let us wade in the river. It was fun and besides, with our big family, no way could Daddy afford a restaurant meal. We always took our food, drove through the park, stopped at overlooks to take pictures, and stopped when we were hungry for a picnic. Our favorites always included homemade pimento cheese for sandwiches and vanilla wafers spread with cream cheese.

This year we were all together and had an eventful time. First of all, the boys were not happy riding on those curvy roads in the heat, no air conditioning in the station wagon. The South had not been completely revolutionized by chilled air blowing through vents. During Southern summers, we all had to deal with the heat indoors and out. All vehicles were not air conditioned, neither were all stores or businesses. We girls in the second seat refused to roll the windows down more than two inches, didn't want to mess up our hair. At one point, the boys were turning pale from the heat and the back and forth on the mountain roads. Altitude didn't help their predicament, ears popping, we all started to chew gum. They grumbled so much we finally relented somewhat and rolled the windows down a little more. Honestly, I was afraid they were going to be sick if they didn't get some air.

Every few miles, Daddy would pull into an overlook and we would all pile out of the car, take a few pictures and allow the boys time to breathe in cool mountain air. The stopping often is probably what saved them from throwing up on us girls. If they had, I'm sure they would have considered it sweet revenge because of our refusal to roll the windows down. Regardless of the boys' seating complaints, we all had fun. The road through the Park pretty much followed the swift flowing Little Pigeon River, so we were allowed to wade in the water often. It was not deep, just swift flowing with a very rocky river bed. That, I believe, was our favorite thing.

Of course, no drive through the park was complete without a stop at New Found Gap and Clingmans Dome. It was a half mile south of New Found Gap and a steep climb along a paved walkway. There were benches beside the walkway for older folks to stop and rest. We kids reached the observation tower at the top without stopping to rest, we were young. Momma and Daddy got there eventually. There was a sloping walk around the cement structure at the top and on a clear day, you can see one hundred miles. This is Clingmans Dome, not only the highest point in the park, but the Appalachian Trail crosses there and it is the highest point along the trail from Georgia to Maine. I know from being there on numerous occasions the view is magnificent.

It was always expected and necessary for all us children to visit souvenir shops and buy something special to take home. The boys leaned more towards Indian headdresses and flimsy bows and arrows. We girls always bought something we thought would last. I personally bought a coin bank made of cedar with a plump black bear sitting on top. There was a slogan printed on the side something about "just like this little bear full of honey, add your pennies and you'll have a bank full of money," surprised I don't still have this, that's why I don't remember the entire slogan. But I do have a cedar box with padlock that holds my diary from long ago. On top of this box is printed Cherokee, N.C., still have the key for the flimsy padlock.

Daddy and Momma always gave us a few dollars to purchase whatever we wanted to take home. This year they decided we were old enough, if we stayed together, to be dropped off and shop until they came back to pick us up. They went back to Craig's Motor Court where Grandma was waiting. We did all our shopping, stood around waiting and waiting until we were all tired of waiting.

Willette was the most irritated and said, "I'm tired of waiting, let's walk back to the house. This is ridiculous, let's go," and she headed in the direction of downtown Cherokee and our rented bungalow.

Of course, we were all tired of standing beside the road, so we followed her lead and headed in the same direction. After walking about half a mile, Daddy and Momma passed us, turned around, pulled over for us to get in. We were all grumbling about having to wait so long after shopping, Willette, in particular, but after we said our piece, we were just glad to be riding instead of walking.

We had all pooled a little money to buy Grandma something. Big Steve, in his comedic role, had purchased a whoopee cushion, which he promptly blew up and discreetly placed in Grandma's chair. She unknowingly sat on it, and made no sign of noticing the sound of what she called 'breaking wind.' Of course, the two Steves were rolling in laughter on the floor. Grandma did not even acknowledge their laughter. She thought it was her making the noise and was not at all embarrassed.

Her gift, a coffee mug, we all innocently contributed to. When we gave it to her, she smiled, looked in the bottom of the mug and haltingly read the message, "Off- your- butt-and- back- to- work." We honestly had no idea that was printed in the bottom. We all had a good laugh over that, except for Grandma. My Grandma was never a joking person, or maybe, she just didn't find it as funny as the rest of us.

8. 1965 School and Big Changes

In August of 1964, I entered the Eighth grade at Pelion High School. We now had a new gymnasium and were thrilled. We still used the old auditorium for school plays, talent contests, beauty pageants, and any important school meetings. The folding metal chairs could now be left in rows in the Auditorium. Mr. Crouch wouldn't have to set them up every time an event was scheduled.

The new gym was for basketball games with fancy bleachers that folded up when not in use. There was a nice lobby with rest rooms, concession stand where snacks were sold through a window with an accordion, fold up metal curtain. There were glass double doors on the front and cement steps down to the sidewalk. All concessions were managed by members of the Beta Club. Students from sophomore to seniors could qualify for the Beta Club if they were smart enough.

The first class to have graduation ceremonies in the new gym was the class of May 1965.

My older sister, Louise, was a member of that class.

There was a slanted tile incline from the original locker rooms, attached to the old auditorium. The incline sloped gently up to the new gym. Right before ball players passed through the double door at the top of the incline, there was a large window that faced the street and short steps that led to a room adjacent to the stage of the auditorium. This room and the one on the other side were considered backstage. Performers waited in the wings here before going on stage. A closet for sports equipment was at the base of the incline along with two locker rooms, each with metal lockers attached to the wall that players could secure with combination locks for their personal items. Across from the wall lockers were showers for the ball players to clean up after a sweaty basketball game. Of course, I never entered the boy's locker room, I strongly suspect theirs were the same as the girls. These old locker rooms were used for the new gym as well.

The graduates of that 1965 class would have dressed in their robes in the old locker rooms, vying for a turn in front of the only mirror. Senior girls primping, fixing their makeup, adding an extra coat of lip color, maybe some blue eye shadow before putting final touches on their hair. Naturally they had to make sure their hair was perfectly brushed, teased so as not to be too flat, and sprayed lavishly with Aquanet before securing the mortar board with bobbie pins. Only then exiting, crossing in front of stage and through the old vending room. They were lined up alphabetically outside to enter the lobby of the new gymnasium. That's the way our class of 1969 did it and senior classes since, as long as the old high school was used. The new gymnasium gave us panther pride every time we were there.

The processional marched slowly down the aisle and sat in orderly rows at the front. A lectern and a table held their diplomas. I know I attended the ceremony and a small reception afterwards in the cafeteria, but don't remember the order of the program.

Every Life Tells a Story

* * *

That summer of 1965, we also went on a vacation as a family, a planned a trip to White Lake, North Carolina and to Wilmington to visit the battleship, the USS North Carolina. Arnold, Louise's fiancée, and his mom and dad were with us. They liked to vacation at a place called Marshburn's beach along the edge of White Lake. We all were standing at the edge of the water, maybe White Lake, and most of us were wearing a sweatshirt with White Lake emblazoned across the front in a photo I have seen.

There is also a picture of Big Steve and me sitting on the Battleship the USS North Carolina's huge anchor. Brother Steve was always the picture of a sharp dressed man. In the photo he is wearing a checkered button up shirt, plaid shorts, neither had the same color scheme, dark loafers with dark crew socks and a stripe around the top. I don't think he was really particular if things matched or not. Sitting on the anchor, I am wearing my White Lake sweatshirt, black with white letters. I guess that is a good indication we went to White Lake then took the trip to Wilmington and the USS North Carolina.

1965 became a very special year in my life. My life would change forever. I fell in love.

9. Fireworks for Life

It was Sunday, July 5, 1965. The day our fireworks began. It was the summer after I completed the eighth grade. I was still only thirteen years old. Having a birthday in October made me one of the youngest in my class. It had been a good year for me. I was a member of the Science Club, played clarinet in the marching band, and sang in Chorus. We called it the Glee Club. My grades were good, mostly A's, maybe a few B's. History was my favorite subject and Billy Gene Stone my favorite teacher. However, I was glad to be out of school for the summer.

I can remember distinctly what happened the day before. It was of course, July 4th, and the reason I remember is because it always happened this way. My daddy got up at dawn to go to Jackie Hite's BBQ in Batesburg and stood in a long line to buy BBQ pork. He would buy several pounds, if available, and hash to go with the rice Momma Jeanette would make for our Independence Day dinner. He always did that on the 4th of July. Momma Jeanette was a great cook and would make rice, potato salad, and several other side dishes. But the BBQ had to come from Jackie Hite's and daddy had to get there early.

The three boys; Donnie, Big Steve, and Little Steve, were outside after dark on the 4th every year. They were in charge of the fireworks display. We girls (Louise, Willette, Lula Mae, Linda, and I), Momma, and Grandma were just spectators. Daddy was there to supervise only. The boys had bottle rockets, roman candles, and lots of firecrackers. Donnie, the same age as myself, lit the fire crackers. One must have had a really short fuse. It burst in his hand. He came inside holding his right hand in his left and was in terrific pain. But Donnie was brave and didn't cry, even though the torture was apparent on his face.

The next day, Sunday, July 5th, 1965, I would meet someone who would change the rest of my life, my future husband, Jimmy Widener. I had had a couple of boyfriends, but he was the one. After dinner on that Sunday, Johnny and Betty Reese stopped by to visit. They had been married only a few years and were visiting Uncle Eugene, Grandma's brother, and his wife Aunt Ethel. They were Betty's parents. Johnny and Betty asked me if I would like to go home with them and spend the week. Since school was out, my daddy said that it would be okay if I wanted to go, and I did. We kids had chores and they multiplied in the summer. We took turns cleaning up the kitchen after meals. During school we only had supper dishes but, in the summer, we had three meals a day to clean up after. We each had kitchen duty, "KP", every other day.

I had never been to this little place called Montmorenci. I had only been to a town nearby called Aiken once. I was really excited to go. They rented a spot for their mobile home on property belonging to Mr. Venning. Johnny's uncle, J.A. Widener, was the overseer for Mr. Venning's large farm and the cattle. Mr. J.A. lived on a lot he had purchased from Mr. Venning and had built a nice brick home that he and his family had moved into three years before. Jimmy was J.A. and his wife, Peggy's son.

On the way to Montmorenci that night, Johnny mentioned his brother, Dean. He never mentioned this first cousin, Jimmy. When we got to Montmorenci, we crossed highway 78, the railroad track, and then pulled into the yard of a brick house. Johnny said, "I'll only be a minute. I need to see if Jimmy can take Betty to Aiken tomorrow to pay our light bill. Y'all can wait in the car. I'll be right back." Betty didn't have a driver's license.

In less than ten minutes, he returned and drove over to their trailer. We three got out. Johnny wanted to show me his corn, so he left the headlights turned on. He was proud of his garden, especially his corn. Standing there in the headlights, we heard a loud boom coming from the direction of the Widener's house.

"Jimmy must be shooting fireworks," Johnny said and answered with a whoop.

Less than a minute later, cousin Jimmy appeared, taking the path that ran from his house to Betty and Johnny's trailer. He was a tall, skinny guy, with black hair and those thick framed glasses that were so popular in the 60's. He was wearing Bermuda shorts and a tee shirt that were both still damp. He explained the wet clothes were from a trip to a small pond he called Gum Springs earlier in the evening where he had been gigging for bull frogs. He said that he had dropped the spotlight over the side of the boat accidently. The spotlight drifted down to the bottom with the light still shining, so he hopped into the water to retrieve it. Johnny introduced me to his cousin Jimmy while we stood there in the headlights. I'll always remember the first thing he said to me, "What a nice place to meet you, in the corn patch."

Jimmy didn't go inside with us that night, but I saw him every day of the following week. He came to take Betty to pay the light bill the next day and I, of course, went along. He was polite and I liked him right away. Evidently, he liked me too. We would sit and watch TV and talk. I said silly things that girls my age had a tendency to say. Things like, "makes you wonder don't it?" or "you can't see through muddy water." I suppose these were responses to some of his questions. It's been so long ago. I can't remember all of the details.

One night, Johnny took me and Betty to the Fox drive-in movie in Aiken. We saw, "Your Cheating Heart," starring George Hamilton. They sat in the front of their red Volkswagen Bug and I sat in the back.

Johnny said, "I'll ask Jimmy if he wants to go with us to a movie tomorrow night. We can go to the Valley Drive-in."

This turned out to be our first date. I was really excited. I wore a pink sleeveless sundress with a white lace insert in the front. The dress belonged to Willette. We girls always shared clothes with each other. Jimmy showed up in yellow plaid Bermuda shorts and a collarless Hensley shirt. We did go to the drive in and saw, "The Carpetbaggers" with George Peppard and Carroll Baker. It was an adult romance, but I don't remember too much of the storyline.

Jimmy kissed me that night. I had never been kissed before, not on the mouth, only on the cheek, by a guy. On the way home after the movie, he was kissing me when a song came on the radio. It was, "Save Your Heart for Me" by Gary Lewis and the Playboys. That kinda became our song.

After I went back home, I didn't see Jimmy again until November. That is when Grandma, Aunt Ethel, Uncle Eugene, and I went to Montmorenci to visit with Betty and Johnny. Jimmy took me uptown to get a hamburger at the A&W Root Beer stand. There were no fast-food chains in Aiken in 1965, only the Snow Cap, Mr. Quik, and the A&W Root Beer stand. The southside of Aiken was still mostly farm land.

Jimmy and I started dating regularly in 1966, he came every Sunday after Church. Often, he took me to a matinee at the

Cinema Theatre on Lauren Street. That allowed us to be back to my house in time for Sunday night church.

We dated for four years. I have saved all our letters to each other. It was too expensive to call long distance back in the sixties. Jimmy graduated in 1968 from Aiken High School and moved to Charleston for a year to go to school. I graduated from Pelion High School in 1969 and one month after graduation, on June 28, 1969, we were married. We celebrated our fiftieth anniversary in 2019.

Jimmy often says, "When I saw you again in November 1965, four months after our 1st date, I couldn't believe the change in your appearance! You had changed from cute to beautiful and I often wondered what did you see in me? You could have had any guy you wanted to date, but you chose me."

There have been lots of fireworks since we met in 1965, good times and bad times, but we have stayed together. We have had three children and three grandchildren. He's still the love of my life, fireworks and all.

I gave my heart away to that tall, skinny guy with the raven hair, black rimmed glasses and dark brown eyes and I never got it back.

10. Courtship

Jimmy and I started dating steady in 1966. He would come every Sunday, after church and we would sit on the back-porch swing and talk, 'just a swingin.' He was always very polite, not just to me, but my whole family. Most Sundays, he took me to the Cinema movie theater for the matinee. He drove a dark blue Volkswagen Bug. At first, he only had restricted licenses and couldn't drive after 6:00 P.M. but he broke the rules driving through the country roads at night after we got home from Pine Grove Baptist Church.

We finally got a telephone in our house about this time, but it was very expensive to call long distance, and of course it was a party line. For those of you that have not had the pleasure, there were four or five families that shared our phone line. You might pick up the phone and someone could be in deep conversation. You did not say things you didn't want your neighbors to hear, because you never knew who was privy to your conversations. Some people would eavesdrop, not us, not intentional anyway. Momma still has the same phone number that we were assigned in the mid-sixties. The party line business didn't last too long and everyone was changed to a private line. But long distance was still expensive and where Jimmy lived in Montmorenci, near Aiken SC, was not local.

Jimmy never called, but after we started seeing each other

regularly, he would write me a letter. I looked forward to Wednesdays; there was usually a letter from him on top of the television, propped up against the clock, so I would be sure and see it. It was mailed on Monday and received on Wednesday.

As you may have surmised from the quick mail service, the postal service took their motto seriously back then. There was no internet, social media, cell phones, not even zip codes. Most marriages were community affairs, transportation was not easy, for long distance romance, postal service was very important, not so today. Couples were introduced by relatives or went to school and church together, making it a high probability that they were related. I became interested in genealogy in my early twenties and found Jimmy's great grandmother, Novie, and my Grandma Florence were first cousins. Jimmy and I are 3rd cousins, once removed, not too close, just like Elvis's song 'Kissing Cousins'. I have found it is really a small world. More about that later.

Montmorenci had a post office, a country store, and an old filling station owned by the Bodie family. There were also some nice homes where the Venning, Mr. Murrel, and Miss Eunice lived. It was a two-story residence, still standing, but now it is a bed and breakfast. Mr. Theodore and Bessie Weeks lived in a huge antebellum sort of house across the highway and close to the post office. The Venning and Weeks families were very wealthy and owned a couple of city blocks in downtown Aiken. I know this because Jimmy's father, J.A. was the overseer of Mr. Murrel's farm in Montmorenci and made repairs on some of buildings he owned in Aiken. Jimmy's Mom and Dad, bought a fairly large lot from the Venning family and built a nice brick home there in 1962.

Back to the story about dating and the letters. I wrote Jimmy too and I still have all our letters. Sometimes when I got home, I would eagerly take my letter, rip it open, and lay across the double bed Linda and I shared and read the letter from him. I would usually write a couple of pages in return and put it in the mailbox for the mail man to pick up the following day. Of course, we had to put the red metal flag up on the side of the box as a signal there was a letter to be posted. Stamps back then were 5 cents and it didn't require weighing. Daddy always had stamps to mail all his payments, so I got one from him. I was always excited to get a letter, but sometimes I had to watch Dark Shadows first, with Barnabus Collins. It came on every week-day at 4:00, almost exactly when the bus dropped us off from school. We would hurry inside, put our books in our room, and plop down in front of the TV. We were all hooked on Dark Shadows and didn't want to miss an episode.

Jimmy and I saw each other almost every weekend through the summer of 1966 and the following year. That first Christmas, I bought him a pink shirt and pink socks to match. I just knew they would look so good with that raven hair of his. He gave me a cameo necklace and earrings.

We frequently went to Montmorenci to visit his parents and little sister, Charmayne. There was a camper size trailer parked among the huge oak trees beside their house. Jimmy's Grandpa Johnnie Widener lived in the camper trailer, he was a big man with blue eyes and blonde hair, inherited from his German ancestors. Grandpa Johnnie was living in the camper in their yard the first time I came and spent the week, that summer of 1965 when I met Jimmy. Grandpa saw me then and when I came back four months later. As Jimmy phrased it, I had changed so much, from cute to beautiful. Grandpa Johnnie must have noticed a change too. At that visit, I walked with Jimmy to his parent's house. Pa was in the yard.

Jimmy said, "Pa you remember Kathy, she stayed with Johnny and Betty last summer."

Grandpa's reply, "Well, she sure looks better than she used to." Jimmy assured me he was only kidding, but I'm not so sure.

Behind Grandpa's trailer was a small fenced area and shelter where Charmayne's pony, Toni, lived.

I never had a long conversation with Jimmy's Grandpa, but they were very close. Jimmy and his cousin, Dean, would spend the night with Pa in his small trailer and from Jimmy's memories, Grandpa Johnnie was a wonderful storyteller and I could tell he was special.

I spent a lot of Sunday afternoons, when we didn't go to the movies, with his family. They were very kind to me, in fact the first Christmas we dated, I received a gift from his Mom and Dad. It was a mirror tray. I, of course, still have it, even though the mirror was broken once, we had it replaced.

* * *

In the Spring of 1967, Jimmy and I remained a couple, seeing each other almost every weekend, even on Wednesday nights. Sometimes, he would show up to take me to choir practice and weekly prayer service.

Valentine Day fell on Sunday that year of 1967 and I was hoping he would remember me with a valentine, maybe a small heart-shaped box of chocolates. Momma Jeanette always made Daddy a red velvet cake, two layers with cream cheese icing, using heart shaped baking pans. I wanted to make Jimmy a cake too.

Momma said, "That will be fine, I'll help if you need me to."

So, the day before, I diligently worked on a heart-shaped, one-layer, red velvet cake for my sweetheart. I even decorated it with M&M's. I was so proud of my efforts and was looking forward to Jimmy's response.

Jimmy drove up on Valentine's day in the blue VW beetle. We had already finished dinner and had the kitchen cleaned up. I peeped out the window to see the lanky, tall, black haired guy I was so crazy about walking toward the front door. He was totally empty handed, no valentine or box of candy. I couldn't believe he had completely forgotten, I decided then and there, I would not give him the cake I made.

He knocked on the door and I opened it, probably not looking as cheerful as usual. He immediately said, "Oh, I forgot, I left something in the car."

When he returned, he was carrying a huge box wrapped in white paper decorated with silver and gold dots and splashes.

"This is for you," he said. "I bet you thought I had forgotten today is Valentine's, but I didn't really."

I was so happy, we walked into the kitchen and I opened the box. It was a 2lb box of miniature Schrafft chocolates. The heart shape box was covered in folds of gold satin ribbon and white lace, a huge gold velvet rose nestled on top with gold satin loops underneath. Around the base of the heart shaped box was scalloped gold cardboard with more folds of gold ribbon and lace. It was the fanciest box I have ever seen, even to this day. That's why I have kept it all these years and the paper it was wrapped in.

It was so beautiful. I knew he must really love me. It had to be very expensive. I gave him his red velvet cake decorated with M&M's.

11. Basketball Games and Honors

In 1967, I was a Sophomore, doing well in school, a member of the Beta Club, FHA, and was honored to be chosen as Miss Sophomore. Wayne Hutto was our class president and placed the crown on my head, kissing my cheek. I kept that crown for many years. It was made from white poster board. The crown part was elaborately shaped, glue covered, then sprinkled with lots of silver glitter. The one-inch-wide band had long extensions on either side, after being cut from the poster board, the band could be folded to form a circle. Presto, a crown and a pretty darn good looking one at that. For every beauty queen the crown was different. Miss Senior and Miss Pelonian were much taller and more elaborate, all made with white poster board, glue, and silver glitter.

We had a beauty contest that year in the old auditorium with judges. I wore a simple unadorned red brocade sleeveless gown. Louise had made it for Lula Mae. Almost all the girls in my class participated, about twelve of us. There were two runners-up for 1st place, all wore long evening gowns and elbow length gloves.

* * *

I loved basketball games on Friday nights. Jimmy would come and take me or Donnie would drive. Daddy was working second shift. Sometimes, Willette and Lula Mae, being cheerleaders, had a boyfriend who took them to home games. Away games, the team, coach, and cheerleaders went together on a school bus.

Coach Rawl taught me P.E. that year. I hated that class, but it was a required course to graduate. We didn't take Physical Ed every day, I think, it was just twice a week. All the girls had to wear this bright blue, short, one-piece jump suit with a belt sewn to the center in the back. This cloth belt cinched the waist with two metal rings attached at the end. The excess belt was threaded through and wrapped under the second ring to keep it in place.

We would do exercises, run laps around the gym, side saddle hops, squat jumps, sometimes played volley ball. I really hated the squat jumps, we had to extend one foot in front, squat down, hands laced behind our neck, then immediately jump back up, change position with the other foot extended, back down and up. There was a certain number we had to do every time we had our PE class and for days after, the calves of my legs were very sore. We also had to sit on the floor, spread out legs, twist at the waist to touch the opposite foot, left hand to right foot and right hand to left foot. The worst requirement was climbing the thick rope, this was to be our final exam. It was attached to the steel brace of the open ceiling. We were supposed to climb up, touch the beam, then slip down on the rope to the floor. Forget that, I couldn't have climbed that rope hand over hand to the top if I was being chased by a bear. Well, I got a C+ as my yearly grade, trust me, Coach Rawl gave me that grade, I surely didn't earn that. I barely got off the floor trying to climb that rope.

At the front of the gym was the coach's office. There was a large window, just glass, so the coach could see what was going on inside the gym and who was doing what on the gym floor. His desk faced this window. He had a good view of the gym anytime he was in his office.

* * *

The school year August 1967 to May 1968, I was a junior and a cheerleader. Vickie Shumpert was our head cheerleader and the only senior on the cheering squad that year, the rest of us were juniors. We practiced some days after school when the gym wasn't being used for player practice. That year, the cheerleaders got new uniforms. The uniforms were much more stylistic than the old vest and pleated skirts. Our uniforms had a bibbed skirt with gold pleats. They were much shorter than the old ones and we had matching silky bloomers that we wore over our undies, so they were considered more modest. We did not do handstands or make a pyramid, nothing fancy, no cart wheels or throwing anyone into the air. We did have pom poms and pranced up and down in front of the cheering section. I still remember some of those cheers and the synchronized moves we made. On the bib top was the letter P in maroon and gold. We wore a white long-sleeved blouse underneath.

Sometimes after home games, we could talk the principal, Mr. Nichols, into having a sock hop. He was always there to supervise along with Coach Rawl and a couple of teachers. We were young and loved to dance. Jimmy would slow dance with me, he didn't like to dance to anything fast: shag, twist, mash potato, or watusi. Every song in the sixties had its own dance, the jerk, the swim, hokey pokey, and of course, everybody loved the limbo rock. After the homecoming game, we always begged for a sock hop.

Kathy Widener

* * *

Every basketball game, when I cheered, was fun. We were a small school, but like all schools, there is one team we just had to beat. In sixties basketball that team was the Gilbert Indians. They were the most important team to beat and we played them every year.

We had an away game at Gilbert High School in 1967/68. Basketball season started in November and ended in February. Every time we had an away game, the bus driver was from Fairview. I remember Beasley Shumpert did most of the driving. If the driver was local, he could pick up all the players and cheerleaders in our small community, then drive to the school, pick up the coach and the Pelion players. After the game, Beasley took the team back to Pelion and took the Fairview kids home. It was normally after midnight before we got home.

That year, the Pelion Panther vs. Gilbert Indians would be an event to remember.

When we got to Gilbert High, we all marched into the gym, players went to their locker rooms and the cheerleaders took position on the away side of the gym. There was a goodly number of Pelion parents and students on our side of the gym. Gilbert was not too far away and this was the most important game every year. Gilbert was the team to beat.

The girls played first, I don't remember the winner, but the boys' game, I do. There were five players in the boys' game at once, sometimes Coach Rawl would call time and send in different players. I remember it was really close for the boys' team.

There was a beautiful pencil drawing of an Indian, regaled in a magnificent headdress. I don't know who did the drawing, but it had to be some very talented student from Gilbert High. The drawing was on fairly thin paper, not on thick poster board, but the size was about the same. The drawing was taped to the block wall of the gym underneath the electronic scoreboard.

It was an exciting and harrowing game. Gilbert was ahead, then Pelion took the lead, it was back and forth throughout the whole game. We were cheering our hearts out. When the final buzzer sounded, the Pelion Panthers were triumphant. Every Panther fan was jumping up and down, yelling, hugging, and laughing. We had beat the Indians! One of the players, Jerry, in his exuberance ripped that beautiful drawing in half. It was in the heat of the moment, but not a wise decision.

The Gilbert fans disappeared fast. There was an unmistakable undercurrent of anger in the air. The girls' team, already changed into street clothes and were waiting with us cheerleaders on the bleachers. The gym was almost completely empty. The Pelion boys' team was still in the locker room changing. Coach Rawl and the boys finally appeared, still grinning from ear to ear. We all, coach in the lead, headed for the exit. The doors were locked. Gilbert students congregated outside the entrance to the gym. Someone had locked us in. There was law enforcement, I don't remember how many officers but it was a very touchy situation.

When the door was unlocked, supervised by law enforcement, Coach Rawl cautioned us, "Do not say a word until we are all back on that bus! No matter what is said to you, do not reply."

It was really a kinda scary situation. We all thought it was not so much that Pelion won the boys' game, it was the ripping of their Indian drawing. Jerry did not destroy the Indian maliciously, it was just in the heat of the moment, winning over our arch enemies in such a close game.

We walked single file to the bus, weaving in and out of the Gilbert people. They made no attempt to open a path for us. No one said a word until we were all safely on our school bus and on

Kathy Widener

the way home. Nothing was said about what occurred or who was responsible for locking us in the gym. We of course laughed and cut up on the way home. That was the most memorable basketball game I cheered at or attended. Go Panthers!

12. Young and in Love

At sixteen, the world was beautiful, especially if you're in love. Every time, I was with Jimmy, he made me feel like a princess.

"Life itself is the most wonderful fairy tale." Hans Christian Andersen

Our relationship felt like a fairy tale. He always made me feel special, never ordinary. For my sixteenth birthday, he gave me a card and some expensive perfume. It was a fancy little bottle, L'air Du Temps perfume by Nina Ricci. There was a little bird on the cap and it smelled absolutely heavenly. Of course, I still have the card and the little perfume bottle.

He took me to my Junior-Senior prom.

The prom was held May 17, 1968 at the Redwood Cafeteria in Columbia, South Carolina. Every couple was dressed to the nines, at least in our minds. Jimmy wore a white sports coat, black tuxedo pants, black bowtie, and presented me with a corsage of pink carnations. He was so handsome and I felt like Cinderella, without the fairy godmother or the fancy coach. Our mode of transportation was a white 1965 Mercury Comet. But it certainly was a magical starry night.

I wore a white slim fitting, sleeveless evening gown with a sheer silky chiffon overlay. I didn't save that, but after fifty-two years, no way could any female still fit more than one leg in a size 6 evening gown. Unless they have an extremely high metabolism or an eating disorder. I have neither. I have lots of pictures and a 5x7 taken by a photographer. My hair was teased and sprayed into a bouffant on top of my head. Willette did my hair. By then, she had graduated high school, married, and was training in beauty school in Columbia.

I do have the handmade program that was given to every attending couple. That's how I know the exact date of the prom, the name of the band, and the menu. The program has a pink cover, two holes punched on the fold and a piece of pink yarn threaded through and tied in a little bow. There was a very talented band called The Classics from Lexington, SC. Our dinner was filet mignon. After the meal, we all hit the dance floor and had a wonderful time. I remember well the band playing Wipeout and lining up for the Limbo rock.

The program stated the Prom was presented compliments of our parents and the Master of Ceremonies was my classmate, Fennis Livington, a junior. In the back there were several blank pages dedicated to autographs. I have those pages full of notes and signatures. Jimmy wrote a sweet note in the back. When I read it to him recently, he remarked, "Did I actually write that by myself." Spelling has never been his forte, but there were no mistakes, it was very sweet.

* * *

Jimmy has always been a very thrifty person. Always had a job and saved his money, but didn't appear ever to mind spending his money on me.

Growing up, he worked on the farm beside his dad and was

paid like all the other farmhands. When we met, he worked at the Hobby House Marine after school most days, then went to work for the A&P grocery store. Always good with budgeting, he never expected me to pay for anything.

I went to work on Saturdays at the Cato ladies wear store on Oak Street in Batesburg. Daddy would take me to work, Jimmy was always waiting to take me home. My friend, Nancy, worked across the street at Dodd's five and dime. It was much nicer working for Cato because the shop was air-conditioned. There was a sign on the door featuring a penguin and the message, 'come in it's cool inside'. Business was good in the muggy, hot days of summer when ladies could shop without sweat trickling down their back. I made about $1.60 per hour, minimum wage at the time.

One Saturday, Jimmy picked me up and took me to Collins Jewelry store around the corner. He bought me a cameo ring, 10k gold and cost $12.00. It was for no special occasion, he just wanted to get me a present.

* * *

A muggy, sunny day, I stood in a long line. Over to my left, I saw for a brief moment, a ghostly apparition, a beautiful dark-haired young girl. Her long white frilly skirt so long and full it gathered in bunches on both sides of the straight back chair and brushed the brick porch floor. She was sitting before a background of large columns and white bricks. Two handsome young gentlemen bending over her upturned face were vying for her attention, laughing at her refusal to save all her dances for them. It was just a vision but I could revisit it in my mind. I had read her angry words more than once. "War! War! War! is ruining all the parties this Spring." The beginning of Margaret Mitchell's masterful novel, *Gone With the*

Wind, had kept me spellbound on the three occasions I have read her book. My mind was not a thousand miles away, it was over a hundred years in the past. I had never seen the movie. In the case of this famous film, the book was better than the movie. I believe this was the beginning of my thirst for genealogy and the obsession to research my ancestry.

My thoughts returned to the present day, June 6, 1968, Jimmy and I stood in a long line at the box office at Richland Mall cinema in Columbia, South Carolina. The movie had been re-released at select cities across America in 70mm wide screen and full stereophonic sound. It came to the Richland Mall location on February 9, 1968 and was scheduled to run for 17 weeks.

I sat spellbound through the four-hour film. I still have the ticket stubs, ticket cost, two dollars. Jimmy even bought a souvenir program booklet for me. Somethings are too sentimental to trash. These mementos are, of course, in a scrapbook, preserved for my posterity.

* * *

Jimmy picked me up after school in the fall of 1968, time for the fair in the South. It was cooler at night and we were headed to the Augusta Exchange Club Fair in Augusta, Georgia. I loved the thrill of riding the tilt and twirl, the Ferris wheel, and of course a ride called the Bavarian. It was like a roller coaster that went very fast around a big circle with up and down slopes, the back wall had a picture of snowy mountains. After it went forward for a several cycles, it stopped and went backward, same speed.

I had no idea that Jimmy got nauseous riding the fair rides. I didn't even notice when we got off the Bavarian roller coaster that he was not as thrilled as me. He suggested we get some cotton candy or a drink and take a breather. He didn't want me to know and didn't tell me until after we were married. He had thrown up on that back wall as we went by. He said when we got off, the operator yelled, "Get me some rags, somebody got sick," as a guy ran by to clean it up.

"I thought he was coming straight for me," he remarked later. In hindsight, I am sorry that I was having so much fun and he was miserable, he just didn't want to ruin my fun. "Love is like the wind. You can't see it, but you can feel it." Nicholas Sparks

13. Senior Year

Jimmy had already moved to Charleston with some of his friends and was attending a tech school. He and his friends moved into an apartment in Mt. Pleasant called Bayview Apartments. He said they only changed the sheets when they were visibly dirty, scary sounding to me. I went with his parents one weekend in September to visit Jimmy but I did not visit the apartment.

Jimmy said, "Daddy did come inside. He picked up a bottle of Jack Daniels and said, "is this yours?"

"No sir, not mine," Jimmy replied.

He later said, "I'm glad Daddy didn't open the bottle; it was full of pee, one of the other guys, of course, but Daddy would not have been pleased."

Jimmy and I went to Sam Soloman and Company, a wholesale store that weekend. I picked out my engagement ring and band. Two months later, November, Jimmy bought my ring. I think he put it on layaway and made payments for those two months. Now we were officially engaged.

In August 1968, I had started back to school at Pelion as a Senior. Jimmy took me to the fair in the fall and by November, basketball was in full swing again. I was a cheerleader, four of the other girls were seniors, the fifth, my sister, Linda Gunter.

The biggest change my senior year at Pelion was the school was finally integrated. There were seven black students in our class. In this small community, black and white got along well. There were no problems. Brown vs. Board of Education was decided in 1954. Why the school was not integrated earlier, who knows. I have fond memories of our new students. Alwillye and Claude Benjamin were brother and sister. Claude played on our basketball team and was one of the best and a starting player. He was an asset to the team. To my knowledge there was no problems with integration that year. It was a new dynamic, they were like us, with darker skin. There were no black families near where I lived and no black students who rode our bus. I really felt empathy for our new students. They were in the minority and had to leave their school and miss senior year with friends to come to an all-white school. I'm glad everybody got along.

My senior year was good. I did well. I was the president of the honor society, so my grades were good, in FBLA (Future Business Leaders of America) and also was honored to be named Miss Senior. An attractive lady, familiar with beauty pageants, and a former 1st runner-up for Miss South Carolina interviewed all senior girls separately. She chose Miss Pelonian, Bonnie Hutto and myself as Miss Senior. Other class representatives Freshman, Sophomore, and Junior were chosen by class vote.

* * *

We seniors received our class rings soon after school started that fall. There was no ring ceremony, all the rings were exactly the same, just different sizes. This was an important symbol of accomplishment. We all wore our rings with pride. The South Carolina state seal appeared on one side with American and our Palmetto flag; the other side had a panther, our school mascot. The year appears on both sides and Pelion High School around the dark red stone on top with a gold P inset in the stone. My ring still resides in my jewelry box. I wear it on occasion. It's 10k gold and cost $39.95.

Graduation was getting closer and we were all excited.

* * *

High school graduation was scheduled for Wednesday, May 28, 1969 at 8:30 P.M. Things I remember about that evening: white dress under my maroon gown, mortar board secured with bobbie pins, new white patent leather low heel shoes, torturing my feet, and major anxiety because I was assigned to give a speech.

There were thirty-six seniors graduating; senior seats were arranged in rows at the front of the gym. Mr. Helms directed a band concert before the graduation processional. Jimmy took me, then joined his parents in the audience. After the concert, the processional would begin.

As we waited outside, there was a slight breeze stirring the tops of the trees across the street, cooling our heated thoughts. The temperature outdoors was bearable. Excitement and anxiety so thick you could almost cut through the emotions with a sharp word. We were beginning a new chapter in our lives, leaving behind childhood. Happy, but anxious for our future. Sherry, Steve, Donnie, Christine, Bonnie, Linda and myself took part in the program. Before we entered the gym, those participating in the program formed a circle and with bowed heads, holding hands, sent prayers to our God that all would go well. We marched in alphabetically, there were seven chairs to the left of the lectern for the presenters.

We walked hurriedly in time to the Pomp and Circumstance

Graduation March; every guest was standing as we made our way down the aisle and stood before our assigned chairs. When we were all in the proper place, we sat down as one, along with our audience.

Sherry King stood, walked to the lectern, and gave the invocation, invocating God's blessings and mercies on all members of the class of 69. Steve Carey stepped to the microphone and gave his prepared welcome to all parents, staff, and friends. Donnie Gunter, my stepbrother, stepped forward and delivered his speech entitled Security - An Illusion. Not a very uplifting title for the future. These speeches were not written by those presenting them. Mrs. Nichols gave us copies of what we were to say and said, "Memorize this." I have no idea who actually wrote the speeches. Then my favorite part, Christine Gunter sang, "I Gotta Be Me," now this was more upbeat and gave us something to strive for. Next another speech, Freedom - A Motivating Force, presented by Bonnie Hutto. At least the title gave us hope, freedom is always a good thing to talk about.

Next up, the longest five minutes of my life. My speech, Opportunity – A Challenge. I had no part in the writing, but I'm sure none of the ears listening absorbed a message, I didn't and I was the person delivering it.

And I quote the first paragraph: "The American Dream is the culmination of the forces of the great growth period of world history. Out of the search for new horizons – out of the yearning of the human soul for freedom of thought and freedom of enterprise came the America of our ideals."

I venture to say, half of the audience and pretty much the whole class had never felt the yearning of the human soul for freedom of thought and freedom of enterprise and as far as the American Dream being the culmination of the forces of the great growth period of world history. What exactly was this great growth period? It was all vague, not very 'awe inspiring' to any of us. I'm sure those in charge felt we were incapable of writing our own words, too young to have experienced situations that gave understanding to past or future hopes and dreams. But I think they were wrong. I was raised to accept authority and the wisdom of adult words. Never would I have questioned the adults in charge or been bold enough to suggest changes to my speech. Looking back now, I wish I could have heard more words from the heart. Like go forward with your life, live it to the fullest, and be thankful for all you have been given. Be kind to everyone, so one day when your name is mentioned, people will smile. I hope I will always be remembered with a smile. I did know what adversity was and how God is in charge. Abandoned as a child by our mother, raised by a Victorian grandmother and a father who worked to put food on the table, I could relate. My life could have definitely been tragic without adults who, though struggling to clothe and feed us children, raised us to be responsible, independent, and to believe in a higher power.

The last presenter, Linda Patterson, sang "One Little Candle."

Our names were called and each person stood and in an orderly fashion passed by, shook hands with the principal, Mr. Nichols, and he placed our high school diploma into our hands. Diploma in hand, we returned to stand before our seats. We sat again as one and listened to brief closing remarks from our principal. We again stood and marched out to start a new chapter of our life.

I have a good memory, but actually I kept the copy of my speech and the program from that evening. Surprised?

Kathy Widener

* * *

My step brother, Donnie Gunter, and I were classmates. Donnie was a smart guy and a member of the honor society too. He planned to join the Navy and Momma told me recently, she had to sign a form of permission, Donnie was not eighteen until May 1st, so he had already made up his mind. I was so busy concentrating on my own life and my own plans for the future, I did not remember that he had joined so early.

After graduation from high school, Donnie received his orders to report to the Naval Station at Great Lakes, Illinois. It was and still is the largest training installation and the home of the Navy's only boot camp. He left home in early fall of 1969, and did his basic training and advanced training there. After his training was complete, Donnie was assigned to the USS Hoel docked at San Diego, California and knew what his mission would be. When he arrived in San Diego, he had a complete physical; he had been having headaches and trouble with his vision. The test was not good. The Physicians diagnosis was a brain tumor and the Navy contacted Momma and Daddy and requested they fly to San Diego for Donnie's operation. This was sometime in 1972 after arriving at what would be his post on the USS Hoel. That was the first time Momma and Daddy ever flew.

Donnie's brain tumor was removed, he was honorably discharged, and sent home. The surgeon told Momma that he could not get all of the tumor because there were roots going into his brain. He gave Donnie maybe three years. He was in a VA hospital in Columbia, SC when he passed away January 10, 1974. He was twenty-three years old.

Every Life Tells a Story

7th Grade Class Officers — L to R — Stanley Shumpert, Steve Carey, William Lucas, Marion Rish and Kathy Gantt (author)

Pelion High Cheerleaders 1967/68 — L to R — Vickie Shumpert, Bonnie Hutto, Sherry King, Kathy Gantt (author), Cathy Williams and Laura Dunbar

Little Steve and Big Steve — background our house and the 1956 Ford Fairlane

Kathy (author) and Donnie Gunter step brother at Ruby Falls, Lookout Mountain TN

Every Life Tells a Story

Jimmy Widener & Kathy Gantt 1967

L to R — Big Steve, Lula Mae, Louise, Momma Jeanette, Daddy, Kathy (author), Grandma Florence. Front — Donnie and Little Steve. (Car in the background is 1962 gold Rambler station wagon)

Kathy Widener

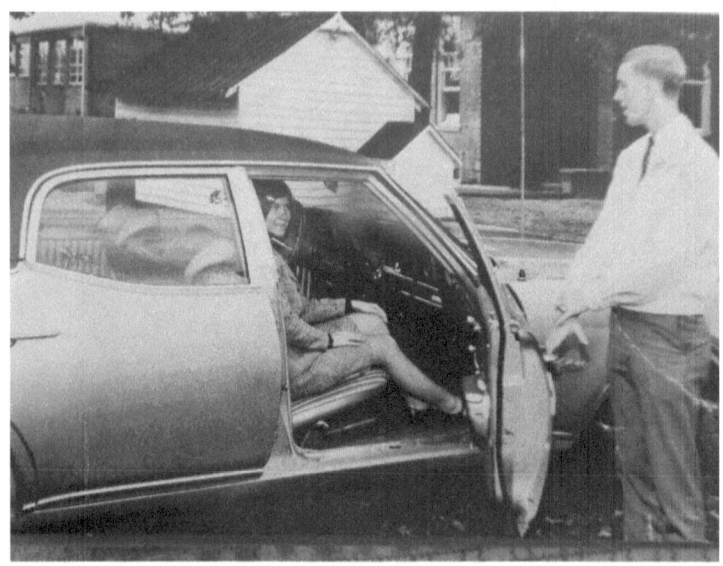

Voted Most Likely to Succeed — Kathy Gantt and Steve Carey

Nancy Shumpert and Kathy Gantt interview Steve Carey for the school paper "The Sandspur"

Every Life Tells a Story

Kathy Gantt (author) — Miss Sophomore

Kathy Widener

Kathy Gantt (author) wading in the Little Pigeon River — Smoky Mountains

Linda, Kathy, Big Steve and Grandma Florence

14. Our Wedding

One month to the day after I graduated from high school, June 28, 1969, I married the love of my life, Jimmy Widener. It was a sunny day, early in the day we had a rain shower and it was steamy by the time of the ceremony, 6:30 p.m. We decided on that time because, as was the custom in the sixties, after six, ladies were not expected to wear hats.

Our engagement had been announced earlier in the Twin City news and mentioned no formal invitations would be sent. All relatives and friends were invited. This was in the 60's, there were announcements placed two weeks before in my church and Jimmy's church bulletins.

Weddings were so much simpler then, no fancy receptions, only nuts, mints, cake squares, and punch colored blue to match the bridesmaids' dresses.

We did have a beautiful three tier wedding cake, made by my friend, Nancy's, mother, Mrs. Laura Bell Shumpert. Daddy took me to pick it up that Saturday morning and I held it on my lap while he drove slowly to the church on bumpy dirt roads. It arrived safely at the church and Daddy helped carry it inside. Miss Laura Bell charged $20.00 for our cake.

We were busy the rest of the morning decorating. All my

sisters and brothers helped cutting ivy and weaving the greenery though the two candelabras rented from Miller's flower shop in Wagener. We also rented a stand to place a beautiful bouquet of flowers between the candelabras, mostly gladiolas, I think. Ivy was also stapled to the base of the step-up choir loft above the pulpit. Tall white tapered candles were put in the holders and were lit by groomsmen before the ceremony. Each of my bridesmaids carried a single long-stemmed white carnation. There were five bridesmaids plus Willette, as my Maiden of Honor. We sisters all took turns as Maid or Maiden of Honor, so each of us had that honor. All the groomsmen, the groom, Jimmy's father as best man, and my Daddy wore rented black tuxedoes. It cost twelve dollars to rent a tuxedo and the shiny patent, laced shoes that were worn with them.

I wore a beautiful lace wedding gown, borrowed from Linda Padgett Harmon. It was so kind of her to loan her gorgeous dress to me and as it turned out, I never needed another.

Every bride has little mishaps and surprises that happen on the wedding day. I had mine too. First of all, one of my bridesmaids lost her headpiece in a home fire, small thing to fix actually. Lula Mae had been in a friend's wedding where blue was the color and had her headpiece from that wedding so Willette, as Maiden of Honor wore the different headpiece. There were two photographers that showed up. I had made arrangements with a photographer in Batesburg, but had tried numerous times to contact him to verify. I could never reach him for confirmation so I hired another photographer. The first photographer had made arrangements for a substitute, but did not tell me. Then there was a problem with wardrobe malfunction, Betty's zipper broke, we pinned that together with safety pins all the way up the back of her dress. No one even noticed. Jimmy forgot to bring a belt to wear when he changed, he just borrowed Mr. Barney Miller's. All men packed their shirts inside their pants, so a belt was needed.

The groom was responsible for the boutonnieres that was pinned to the lapels of his attendants, groomsmen, and the bride's bouquet. I carried a white Bible with a white orchid nestled among satin ribbons that secured the corsage and long streamers of satin ribbon hanging in front.

The wedding was not fancy at all, but it was perfect, with a few little surprises. The really big surprise, I did not realize at the time. My beloved, but difficult Uncle Leon Gantt had donned a suit and tie to be there. He didn't sign the register book and didn't attend the reception, he went to sit in the car, but he came. He had probably only been to one other wedding, his own.

15. Marriage, Living on a Shoestring

We retrieved our 1965 Comet that was parked behind a church friend's house to protect it from vandalism. These were the days of not just tin cans tied to the back of the car, but air let out of tires, open sardine cans on the motor, and toilet paper strung all over the happy couple's car. All of this was in good fun, except for the groom who had to change the tire and remove the other trappings of hilarious jokesters.

Linda and Carlisle Harmon took us to our car after the ceremony. Of course, we had to change to traveling clothes before leaving the church. Jimmy wore a green shirt and green plaid pants with a borrowed belt. I wore a blue checked drop waist dress with pleated skirt, navy wrist length gloves, and navy pumps. Before our hurried departure, facing the opposite direction, I tossed a bouquet over my shoulder for the next lucky bride to catch. My sister, Lu, caught it. She had dropped the Lula Mae when she went to Newberry College.

***

We jumped in our 65 white Comet and headed up highway 178. The interstate system was under construction and I-20 was still dirt between 178 and Lexington. When we got to where I-20 was being constructed we took the unpaved interstate. It was like a dirt race track, smooth and hard packed clay. There were two lanes, no pavement. Construction was being done, but the paving had not gotten as far as highway 178. Locals who wanted to go to Lexington or Columbia used the dirt interstate, no traffic all the way to Lexington. The interstate was paved past there to Columbia, that was where paving had begun. Our wedding trip consisted of a two-night stay in Columbia, South Carolina. We stayed one night at the Holiday Inn, the second at the Tremont Motel. Still have the receipt from the Holiday Inn, cost $12.50 for one night. We were so broke; we couldn't even pay attention. But we were very much in love and we were together, that's what mattered.

Jimmy said, "I came home with one hundred bucks in my pocket, I was happy about that."

After a two-night honeymoon, we came back to Montmorenci and his parent's house. We stayed with them, sleeping in Jimmy's old room for maybe a week until our mobile home was ready to move into. Jimmy approached Miss Rosa and Mr. Roy Summers about an empty spot on their land, two blocks up Woodward Dr on old Dibble Road. They knew Jimmy, he was their paper boy and friends with their grandson, Lenair Hutto. They graduated from Aiken High the same year. The Summers agreed to rent us the spot, with a water hook up, for $25.00 a month.

That's where our mobile home was parked. Grandpa Johnnie had passed away about six months before we married, so his camper trailer was traded as a down payment on our 12x52 feet Statler. Our trailer home was already furnished. The only furniture that we added was my cedar hope chest, a six-foot-long stereo record player Jimmy had purchased in Charleston, and Grandpa Johnnie's portable black and white TV. The trailer was not air conditioned so we bought a window unit from Williston Furniture company and placed it in the living room.

When you stepped into the front door, with roll out frosted glass panes, to the right was the kitchen. There were black saloon doors that could be closed. I don't have a clue why they were added, we always kept them open. The kitchen floor was vinyl and looked like a brick floor. The appliances, refrigerator, stove, and sink were avocado green. There was an oval wooden kitchen table and four spindle backed chairs to match.

In the living room we had an upholstered sofa, two chairs, one was a rocker, the fabric covered pieces looked early American, brown fabric with ruffled skirts on the bottom. There was also a coffee table and one lamp table positioned between the two chairs. My hope chest was placed on the wall that separated the living room from the kitchen and Grandpa Johnnie's twelve inch black and white TV sat there. Maybe the saloon doors and the spindle backed chairs in the kitchen were supposed to add esthetically to the early American motif.

There was bright green carpet in the living room, other rooms had vinyl flooring. There were two bedrooms, one extremely small 8x9 feet with a small built-in closet, two small drawers underneath.

The bathroom also had avocado commode and tub. The sink was one-piece white marble design with wooden base and drawers. A small medicine cabinet with sliding green plastic doors and a mirror was placed above the sink. There was a short wall and a built-in bench with a green cushion. A linen closet was built in between the tub and the wall to the back bedroom. There was a washer inserted in a space in the hall directly across from the back door. The washer was the avocado color, very popular in the 70's along with copper tone and harvest gold. Jimmy had to put clotheslines up in the back yard. We had no clothes dryer. Our bedroom had counter space and built-in drawers all the way across the end of the trailer. There was a closet with two folding metal doors and a shelf above. The bed had no headboard. The mattress was maybe four inches thick and foam, very uncomfortable. We didn't care.

We now had a trailer payment with Georgia Railroad Bank in Augusta. Jimmy's parents made the payment arrangements, we had no credit. Jimmy went back to work at the A&P. I was busy keeping our little home spotless. I was only seventeen, didn't have any transportation, and no driver's license. Jimmy worked out a budget in a red ledger, what we would pay with every paycheck. The trailer payment was $87.12 a month, we had the space rent, electric bill, and all those necessary things. His parents gave us $20.00 a week to buy groceries and Jimmy got busy looking for a better paying job. We even had milk delivery three times a week, two glass quart bottles, placed on the top step at the front door. Our paper boy, Tommy, delivered by bicycle, tossing it in the front yard early every morning. We were definitely what I consider the working poor, but we didn't get any handouts except from his parents, no welfare, no food stamps or health insurance. It seems so long ago now, but how times have changed.

In August 1969, Jimmy was hired at the Owen Corning Fiberglas Plant just three miles up the road. That meant we would have health insurance.

On the way to Aiken one day, after he had started work, we had a conversation about having a baby. I wanted to experience motherhood right away and Jimmy agreed. That was the day he threw my birth control pills out the car window.

Thinking back, I don't know why I was in such a hurry for motherhood. I knew nothing at all about babies, never babysat for any little children. I don't think I had ever held an infant, much less changed a diaper. But I knew I could do it. By the end of October 1969, I was expecting. I went back to visit Dr. McLin in Batesburg, he had delivered me and I saw him growing up. He confirmed that I was indeed pregnant. When I told my daddy the good news about my visit to Dr. Mclin, I don't believe he was as excited as I was.

His respond to my news, "McLin's word ain't no prayer book."

First and only time I heard that, but I could tell he was not pleased. I'm sure he was thinking about how hard it was raising a child, especially with little money and I was so young, not much more than a child myself. Jimmy and I were thrilled.

* * *

This was during the Vietnam War and America had reinstated the draft. A lottery was to be held December 1, 1969. The Selective Service conducted two lotteries to determine the order of call to military service in Vietnam. It would include all men born from January 1,1944 to December 31, 1950. All 366 days of the year, including February 29, were written on slips of paper, each paper placed inside a plastic capsule. All were then dumped in a huge glass container. Jimmy's birthdate, May 11, was the twelfth date drawn. He would have been destined to serve in Vietnam, but that was not God's plan.

The 319th Transportation Company Army Reserve unit headquartered in Augusta, Georgia had just returned from Vietnam. Almost all members who came back from their tour of duty in Vietnam were mustered out of the service. Jimmy was told this by a returning neighbor. He went to Augusta and was able to sign up for the Reserve before he was drafted. He left the 2nd of December 1969 for basic training at Fort Polk, Louisiana. Two weeks later he came home for Christmas, then back to Fort Polk. All the army guys called it Fort Puke, Louseyana. His obligation to the reserve was for six years. After basic, he did AIT at Camp Bullis near San Antonio, Texas. They called themselves weekend warriors.

After Camp Bullis, he would have to attend a weekend drill at the reserve center once a month and attend two weeks of summer camp. Being in a Transportation Company they, of course, would transport supplies in wartime, but on their weekend meetings they were responsible mechanics, checking out all the equipment and keeping it in good working order. The company traveled by convoy to Camp Shelby in Hattiesburg, Mississippi in July every year. Four friends who were about his age joined with him, Ricky, Glenn, Byron, and Wayne.

He was considered regular Army during his training, then received pay for his weekend drills. After he served his six-year obligation, he would be joining for another six, just for drills and summer camp. We badly needed the small check he received every month. He didn't finish the second obligation, but he does have two Honorable Discharges. We definitely lived on a shoestring budget.

16. Motherhood

> "A baby is something you carry inside you
> for nine months, in your arms for three years,
> and in your heart until the day you die"
> —*Mary Mason*

I was pregnant, Jimmy was away serving in the U.S. Army and I did not want to stay in our trailer home in Montmorenci all alone. I was very young and wanted to be near my family. Living with my mother, Sallie, was the best option and she invited me to stay. Daddy and Momma Jeanette still had children at home and my Grandma Florence. I had reconnected with my mother. She had also remarried and had a five-year-old son. Her husband, Palmon Spires, worked at a job in Georgia all week and only came home on weekends. He was a good man and didn't mind that I was staying with Momma.

Momma Sallie took me to my doctor appointments in Columbia, South Carolina. My physician was Dr. Julian Salley, nice guy. I, of course, had no idea what I was having, girl or boy. There were no ultra sounds taken in 1970 to let the mother know the sex of the child. I can remember the first time I heard my baby's heartbeat; it was loud and very fast. I realized that carrying that tiny life inside of me was indeed a miracle.

Jimmy finished his Army Reserve training and flew home from San Antonio on the 24th of April, 1970. I know the exact date because, I still have his airline ticket stub in our scrapbook. He flew Eastern Airlines, San Antonio to New Orleans to Atlanta and Augusta Georgia, cost $40.95. I don't remember going to the airport, his parents probably picked him up, then he came to get me. We moved back into our mobile home, but I still had to go to Dr. Salley in Columbia. My due date was June 24, 1970, but my baby still had not arrived three weeks later. You can imagine, I was ready to have this child. That's when someone, Momma Sallie, I believe, suggested I could drink a bottle of castor oil.

"If you're not ready to have that baby, it won't hurt you, just makes you go to the bathroom a lot, like any laxative."

Taking castor oil is like drinking grease. I did manage to get the nasty concoction down. I guess I was just so tired of being pregnant, I was desperate. I wouldn't have done anything to jeopardize that precious little life, Momma assured me I would be okay. I forced down a small bottle on Friday, July 10. On Saturday, July 11, I did indeed go into labor, late in the afternoon.

Jimmy took me to the Baptist Hospital in Columbia, Momma Sallie and my sister, Louise, were in the back seat for moral support, I guess. A nice little black lady, Miss Lillian, got me prepped for delivery. Of course, my labor took all night and the pain was excruciating. I had always heard that you forget the pain, once you hold that sweet little babe in your arms. That is not true, I didn't forget the pain. It is however true; I definitely decided all the hurt was worth it.

As the hours passed, the labor pains were more frequent and harder to bear; I hardly noticed the gray dawn beginning to lighten the world outside. It was as though the labor pains would never stop. They were coming so fast and I was exhausted. Finally, a nurse checked me and announced I was ready to deliver. All I remember, after that, was being pushed down the hall and into the bright lights of the delivery room. Dr. Salley was beside me and I was being hooked up to an IV line, someone at my head asked me to count backwards from one hundred, I think I made it to ninety-eight and everything disappeared. That's all I remember until I woke up in recovery. I could hear voices but was not able to tell where these voices were coming from. I groaned and a nurse immediately appeared beside my bed.

"Please tell me what I had, boy or girl," I whispered.

She didn't know which. She asked other workers in recovery. "What did Mrs. Widener have?" The answer, "She had a little girl."

I smiled knowing I had accomplished something. The pain was gone and I had delivered a tiny little angel.

They then got me cleaned up, moved to a semi-private room, and allowed Jimmy to come in. Shortly thereafter, my baby was brought to me. Melanie Lynn Widener was born at 6:29 a.m. on Sunday morning July 12, 1970. She was so tiny, she only weighed 5 lbs. 7 oz. and was three weeks past due. Dr. Salley called her post mature. She was just perfect. I counted her fingers and toes and per her pediatrician, Dr. Castles, everything was fine.

At that time there was no such thing as preemie clothes, so even birth to three months size would be way too big. Newborns wore diaper shirts and a cloth diaper with rubber pants over the diaper. There were disposable diapers available, but we could no way afford disposable. There was also a diaper service for more affluent mothers. The service would deliver several dozen clean diapers every week to your home and pick up the soiled ones. Needless to say, we definitely couldn't afford that. My roommate, Betsy, ordered the diaper service, so I was made aware that it was an option. But then, Betsy's husband was the editor of the evening newspaper in Columbia at the time. Thinking back, I spent a week in the room with this woman and if I saw her new son's father at all, I don't remember. Either he made no impression on me or he didn't visit very much. Jimmy came every evening from Montmorenci, fifty miles away.

I had received three or four dozen cloth diapers from my two baby showers, they were cotton in the shape of a square. I don't remember how to fold a cloth diaper now, probably no one else does either, but there was a correct way and I learned. These cloth diapers were pinned on with oversized safety pins which had a little plastic duck or some other little animal for decoration. To prevent pricking Melanie while securing the diaper on either side, I pinned the diaper on with my right hand while slipping the fingers of my left hand between Melanie and the pin. I would have much rather stuck myself than her.

I was discharged on Friday, but Melanie was having some problems with the Enfamil her pediatrician, Dr Castles, had prescribed. They kept her until Monday. The new milk he prescribed was Neomulsoy, which was kind of brown in color; it didn't look at all like milk.

We went back to the Baptist Hospital in Columbia on Monday to bring her home. Allowed into the nursery, a nurse suggested, "Why don't you give her the bottle? It is time for her to be fed again." I even changed her into the little white cotton dress with tucks in the front, her going home outfit. After I gave her half of the four-ounce bottle and sat her up in my lap to burp her, she threw up all over her little white dress and me. Fleetingly I thought, they might not let me take her home, since this milk didn't seem to agree with her either. I put a diaper shirt on her, which was way too big and we were soon on the way.

I had to learn how to sanitize glass bottles on the stove in a big pot of water, change diapers, using cloth diapers and diaper pins. We didn't have a clothes dryer so diapers had to be washed and hung on the clothes line to dry. Sometimes when it rained for several days or longer, I would wash Melanie's diapers and clothes, take them out of the washer, drop them into my wicker laundry basket, and take them to a laundromat to dry in one of their big dryers.

Dr. Salley charged $250 for normal delivery. We had to make monthly payments, so I guess you could say, we had to finance her. I'm sure they would not have repossessed her if we hadn't made the payments. I believe we paid $25 a month until the debt was paid.

* * *

Jimmy went back to work at Fiberglass on the night shift. It was so hot that summer, living in a trailer home, with no shade trees, was sort of like living in a tin can. The outside was metal, walls and roof. In order for Jimmy to sleep in the daytime, he slept on the sofa under the air conditioner with a box fan on the opposite side of the room blowing the cold air back onto him. Sometimes he just slept on the floor. There is a picture of him on the floor, Melanie next to him on a pillow, both sound asleep.

Melanie was such a tiny little thing, but strong. She was walking at nine months and barely weighted twenty pounds. We gave her a pacifier and at first, it was half as big as her little face.

She had a beautiful birch crib with a wooden cutout of a pony on the bottom, Momma Sallie bought her crib. Pretty soon she was standing up in her crib and trying to climb out. The little room was hers and she loved to stand up in her crib and look out the window. Her Papa J.A. would come by every afternoon on the way home and stop to see his baby. As soon as he pulled up in his city work truck, she would snatch the curtain aside and grin at her Papa as he climbed from his truck. She was so excited, she would drop on all fours, crawl and pull up in her crib to watch the door. As soon as he appeared, she reached her arms for him to take her from the crib, beaming at Papa J.A. Melanie was the first grandchild, that designation alone meant she would be spoiled and she was.

Once I came to check on her and Jimmy was in the crib with her. I only wish I had taken a picture of him, long skinny legs all folded up, head laying on a baby pillow. Melanie was sitting up, watching her Daddy as he gave her small toys to entertain her. Of course, they went straight to her mouth. The first thing a baby wants to do is taste everything. She seemed to like her Daddy in her crib playing with her toys, and winding up her music box. Of course, her first word was 'da da'. She was a Daddy's girl.

One night when she was still a tiny baby, she had colic. Her tummy was hurting and she was whinny. Jimmy and I were up all night. We took turns holding her and rocking her to try and soothe her hurt. Finally, just as the daylight began to push back the night, she fell asleep. Jimmy carefully, patting her back all the way and swaying gently, took her to her bed. Then and only then did we go to bed ourselves.

* * *

I spent a lot of time washing baby clothes and diapers. She had her own little clothes hamper in her room. The diaper pail where wet and soiled diapers were deposited was also in her room. Whenever she had a BM in her diaper, I would take the soiled diaper to the bathroom, clean the baby poop out in the commode, wring the water from the diaper and drop into the waiting pail. I washed all baby clothes in a different detergent from our clothes. I washed them in Ivory Snow, powdered detergent especially for delicate fabrics. I don't think it is still available, but in the 70's, it was really popular with mothers, solely for their baby's clothes.

When Melanie was napping in her crib in the heat of summer, I would put a small fan on her little clothes hamper, pointed toward her to keep her cool. Once when her fan was blowing, I changed her diaper, containing a big solid lump of poop. I was thinking how could something so sweet produce something that smells so bad. I took the diaper off, picking it up by the four corners to carefully deposit the smelly stuff in the commode.

I'm sure you can already guess what happened. I dropped one corner of that diaper and the 'shit hit the fan.' There was a brrrr noise and a strip of poop was deposited on the ceiling and around half the room. At first, I was horrified. Then, I started laughing. I couldn't help but see the ramification of an expression I had heard many times.

Jimmy appeared, "What is so damn funny?"

Looking around, he realized what had happened. "Well, I guess the shit really did hit the fan, didn't it?" It took a few minutes for me to regain my composure and Jimmy cleaned the streak of brown off the wall and the ceiling. Thank goodness it was not an oscillating fan; it could have been worse. It was only the walls and the ceiling, none on the crib or Melanie.

17. The 1970's and Style

In August 1971, Jimmy got a new job. He went to work for the Carpet Shop in Augusta, Georgia, selling carpet. He turned out to be a good salesman, not quite the kind that 'can sell ice to an Eskimo', but he was honest and developed a rapport with the customers. He tried to steer people towards their best option, no high pressure sales pitch, therefore people would return and recommend others to him.

* * *

I finally got my driver's license at age nineteen. Daddy took me to Wagener to take the driver's test. I took the test once, failed. The second time I passed. That was the last time I parallel parked a vehicle, fifty years ago. I guess I can forget that now, I had a driver's license, if only I had a car to drive. Jimmy was driving our new Chevrolet Vega hatch back. It was what I consider a poison green. We bought it from Vernon Chevrolet in Aiken, it cost $2,400. Now we had a car payment of $79 a month.

That Christmas, 1971, Jimmy's Momma and Daddy gave me a sewing machine for Christmas. I knew how to sew. Miss Doris Gunter had taught me. Now when Melanie was sleeping, I could sew.

I bought a cardboard accordion cutting board, which I could unfold on our bed, the only flat space available. The material had to be folded in half, positioned on the cutting board and pinned down with stick pins. The pattern was like tissue paper, very flimsy and had to be cut out very carefully. By cutting the pieces out on doubled material, two pieces of each were produced at one time. I started making a lot of Melanie's clothes, mine, and eventually Jimmy's. I haven't sewed in years, but haven't forgotten. I recently discovered that I still have the patterns for my skirt, blouse, and vest I made in Miss Doris's Home Ec. Class. Mainly, the sewing became a way to save more money.

Jimmy and I both did whatever to make extra cash. Once he installed carpeting in a Volkswagen beetle for some customer. A young woman came into the carpet store and purchased a short twist shag and wanted it installed in her VW. That was not something the store crew would do, they only did home installation of carpet, so Jimmy volunteered. I well remember, it was in the hot summer of 1972, Melanie was already asleep in her crib, air-conditioning blasting in the living room and the small fan keeping her cool. Jimmy and I were in the front yard. He cut and glued the carpet down; I held the flashlight so he could work. We didn't finish until about three a.m. He got $15.00 for his labor. The main thing Jimmy remembers was the Beetle came with factory air-conditioning, which was rare at that time.

***

The summer of 1972, we decided to build a house. Mr. Charles Venning agreed to sell us a lot beside the Wideners. It cost us $2,000 for the one-acre lot, that was very expensive at the time, but it was a beautiful lot full of massive hardwoods, mostly oaks.

Our lender, the Farm Home Administration, agreed to finance the building and even the lot.

We found a floorplan we liked, just slightly over fifteen hundred square feet, three bedrooms, dining room, kitchen, one-and one-half baths, and a living room. When it was approved by our lender, we contracted Mr. Buck Jeffcoat of Swansea to build the house. His son, Ray, drew the blue prints.

Jimmy got the shag carpet through the Carpet Shop where he worked. We had shag carpeting in all the rooms, even the bathrooms. The kitchen, utility rooms, and the front foyer floors were vinyl. We also had a shag carpet rake, plastic tines to keep the carpet looking nice. The flooring in the utility room where the washer and dryer were installed was a zebra print, black and white vinyl. Everything was wild in the 70's, even the flooring.

Melanie picked the paint and shag carpeting for her room. She picked out a Pepto Bismol pink for walls and floor. It was so pink, it made me feel a little queasy going into her room, but we told her she could pick out the color she wanted. We should have considered the fact that she was only two and a half and gave her a little more guidance, but we didn't. She was so happy with her new room. She also got a new bedroom suite, a twin bed, dresser, and chest of drawers. Even at her age, not quite three, she was proud of her room and kept it clean, all her toys picked up and the bed made.

We went to North Furniture and bought the furniture for our new house. We bought a black vinyl sofa, chair, and two lamp tables for the den (it had red shag carpet) and floor length dark red brocade curtains with plastic backing. The walls, of course, were dark brown paneling. The kitchen had copper tone appliances, double door refrigerator, and drop in range. The cabinets were constructed by Mr. Jeffcoat's crew. The dining room had an oval dining table and six chairs and a china cabinet (baby blue shag in there). Our room had queen size bed, triple dresser with two mirrors, and nightstand. An attached half bath, sink, shower and commode completed the master suite. The carpet was yellow shag and the shower had yellow tile. We also bought a table and four chairs for the kitchen; the wallpaper in the kitchen was covered with blue tea pitchers. There was one wall of gold and black frocked wallpaper in the foyer and the hall bath had dark blue frocked wallpaper and light blue tub, sink and commode with light blue shag carpeting. Even the tile on the vanity top and around the wall of the tub was white with light blue veins. Welcome to the 70's folks! All the furniture we purchased from North Furniture. Total cost $1,500, so evidently it was of the highest quality? We sent Mr. Drew at North Furniture a small payment every month until it was paid.

We moved into our new house in December 1972. We were indeed proud to have a brick ranch style house. When I envision the décor of our new house now, I almost cringe, but that was the style back then.

* * *

I do believe I should at least mention the clothes of the 70's. When we married, the groomsmen wore normal black tuxedos. In the 70's, we're talking groomsmen with tan tuxes and little blue ruffled front shirts or some other bizarre combination. I myself, well remember wearing very short mini-skirts, purple velvet hot pants, and white go-go boots. Most dresses were made of wild patterned double-knit material. I had shoes that were patchwork suede, block heels, and different patches of off white, blue, purple, grey laced with pink laces. Clothing styles went from bad to worse. I did a lot of sewing and made matching double-knit dresses for Melanie and myself. And how can I forget bell bottom pants.

Guys wore wide lapels in outrageous mismatched checks and plaids. I made Jimmy a mint green leisure suit jacket, went great with his white patented slip-on shoes. Suits tended to be plaid, both jacket and pants, with the most outlandish wide ties. He had a light blue denim jacket, I made, of course. It had cuffs. Made like a denim work jacket, the buttons were brown and for extra effect I embroidered an island on the back with a coconut palm tree (actually has a coconut on it), waves in the ocean, and a beautiful sunset. He still has that jacket hanging in his closet, but to put it in perspective, he has a shirt my Grandma gave him for Christmas. Grandma passed away in 1974. We both are like that, can't seem to part with things that are sentimental.

Sunglasses were huge, covered most of my face, I had long straight hair parted in the middle, we were pretty much the hippie generation, Jimmy wore his hair much longer and even had a full black beard.

When he had to get a new driver's license, he asked the lady at the DMV, "Can I keep this photo?" She agreed and cut it off the license as a keepsake. He really looked more like the Unabomber, but so did a lot of guys. A whole generation that my Grandma and Granddaddy would have never recognized. In the fifties, guys wore their hair in a flat top, the sixties it was neat hair with black rimmed glasses, along came the seventies and long shaggy hair or mullets. Beards were very much in vogue.

In my humble opinion, the 50's & 60's had the prettiest cars, best music, and classiest clothes. I watch movies from that era, just to see the cars and the way ladies and gentlemen dress. The men wore fedora hats, suits, ties, and top coats. Ladies wore heels, dresses, hose, and wrist length gloves. When they went out to dinner or to a dance, they looked fabulous. Very classy.

I didn't realize how degraded style would become. There is no style now. Wear what you want. It's really sad. But unless you're walking the red-carpet or attending a fancy ball, any outfit is accepted, even pajamas and house slippers. Don't even mention the jeans with big holes and rips in the legs. When I was growing up, they would have gone in the trash or used as mechanic grease rags. Who could have guessed how very expensive holey jeans are, simply unbelievable for a 60's girl.

18. Snowstorm of the Century

Two weeks before Christmas 1972, we began the move from our mobile home, two blocks up on Old Dibble Road to Woodward Drive. At this time there were no street names. We had always received our mail through the post office, almost directly across the railroad tracks and Highway 78 from our new home. Our Box # was 23, still is today, however the boxes were not opened with a key, there was a combination lock at first.

Mrs. Laura and her husband, Mr. Vic Reardon, lived in a huge white house right around the corner on a dirt street. Miss Laura was the Postmistress; Mr. Vic was a veteran of WWI and WWII. They had no children, just the big white house, wraparound porch, and a house full of antiques. Miss Laura's father was a medical doctor, Dr. Woodward, her mother was a Northern lady, a Miss Allen, from the north, a Yankee, and was snubbed by the locals. Miss Laura told me her mother's family moved South soon after the War so her father could run the Graniteville cotton mill. She retired from her Postmistress job soon after we married.

***

Barely two months after settling into our new home, what would become the snowstorm of the century in the South Carolina midlands disrupted everything in our state. Steely gray clouds began banking early morning to the Northwest. Big fluffy ominous clouds like dirty dish water consumed the sky spreading from North to South The snow started to fall about 11:00 A.M. on Friday, February 9, 1973. We had no idea what we were in for.

Melanie and I watched from the dining room windows as the snow started coming down, very hard, very fast. The wind blew the tops of the trees, waving them back and forth as though a giant hand gripped the trunk, as a flag waving in gale force wind. The temperature began to drop straight downward and lone oak leaves that still clung to branches of the huge trees in our yard danced in the wind. The weather report was forecasting one to two inches accumulation. I watched through the windowpane in the side door. The big thermometer nailed to a young oak tree not ten yards from the door was visible, the numbers, bold black marking ten-degree increments. The red stripe of mercury apparent, first in the upper twenties, then lowering ever so slightly as the day wound down.

We could only watch as the snow began to cover the front yard. No grass had taken hold yet, but snow accumulated on the patches of centipede that we had planted in clumps in the cleared yard. The trunks of huge oaks standing in the front yard soon had a coating of white, limbs violently whipping back and forth. With the wind whistling and the snow deepening with no let up, everything became white. It was a vivid contrast against the stark darkness of trees bordering the yard's edge. The woods seemed to close in around us, the clearing where the house stood seemed surrounded by a wall of black with the swirling snow obliterating every feature.

We could only watch from the double windows in the dining room or pull aside the thick curtains in the den to watch the storm's progress. I was pregnant with my second child and Melanie was just two and a half. She wanted to go out, but it was too dangerous in the almost blizzard conditions. At times we could barely see the railroad track, the houses, and red barn directly across highway 78. The brick steps, back and side yard, were coated and I was not willing to risk getting a closer look, especially without a rail on the steps. Way back then, there were no cell phones, no internet, and only three local channels on the TV. Jimmy was probably on his way home, but he would have no way to contact me, unless he pulled over at a pay phone. I put Melanie down for a nap, made a cup of coffee, grabbed a book, and just waited sitting by a window peering at the storm. At least we still had electricity. All schools let out early and folks started heading home from work, didn't want to be caught on the roads after dark when the mercury would be plunging into the teens. The roads, especially bridges and overpasses, would be slick with black ice.

Jimmy left work early from his job at the Carpet Factory Outlet, K Mart Plaza in Augusta. The roads were crowded and overpasses were just beginning to freeze. It was late evening when I saw him creeping into the side yard in our green Chevrolet Vega.

"It was really slow going; crowded roads and a mixture of sleet and rain along with falling temperatures, all overpasses and highways are already treacherous," Jimmy announced to me when he finally came inside. "I want to cover the windshield and the back window with tarps before it gets worse. The snow is already beginning to pile high on the hood and it doesn't seem to be letting up. The wipers were flapping back and forth trying to keep the windshield clear enough to see. Boy, am I glad to be home."

The snow whipped and swirled all through the night from 11 a.m. on Friday until late afternoon on Saturday. There were cement blocks standing on end in the back yard by the dogwood trees we had planted. The end of the blocks was barely visible. We were fortunate, we still had electricity and food. All we had to do was hold up until the temperature rose and the sun came out.

Reporting from the local radio and television stations, "strong gusty winds will continue to pump cold air into the state. Thousands of motorists are stranded on snow covered highways. The South Carolina Highway Patrol announced the situation is critical. Helicopters from Shaw Air Force base continues to airlift and emergency rescue occupants, their cars stuck in snow drifts. Forty-eight tractor trailers are backed up at US 321 and I 26 intersection near Columbia."

Many of these stranded motorists were welcomed into homes. I know our neighbors across the highway took in a family of strangers. In a crisis there are good Samaritans to be found. Sometimes the worst of times brings out the best in people.

That Friday evening, Jimmy's Daddy, J.A. got home earlier than usual. His nephew, Losik, had been working with him for the city of Aiken in Streets and Parks. Losik was stranded and would be staying next door. Charmayne, Jimmy's younger sister had her friend, Janet, spending the night. Those three teenagers, Losik, Charmayne, and Janet waded through the snow after nightfall, carrying a flashlight. Only emergency vehicles were using the roads. They made the trip to our house and sat around the kitchen table with Jimmy and played strip poker. They decided that would be more fun than any other card game, but only down to underwear. I, of course, in my condition decided to sit this one out.

We all had a fun time. They didn't have far to go home, so we all stayed up late, eating junk food, laughing, listening to long playing albums on our stereo, enjoying each other's company. It was freezing outside, but there was no disruption of electricity. With lights, heat, and plenty to eat, we listened to the Beatles, Beachboys, Sonny and Cher, Elvis, and Johnny Rivers. I turned the radio to WBBQ, caught the local news and weather updates; we were so fortunate, there was so many people that were not. There was at least one death noted in the Aiken Standard after the storm. The body of a woman was found on a railroad track, she had frozen to death, stranded when her car left the road and ended up in the deep snow of a ditch. Evidently, she had tried to walk to safety.

The next day we awoke to a winter wonderland outdoors. Best observed from indoors in my condition. I didn't want to risk a fall. I do have a picture of Melanie, bundled up beside a giant snowman made by Charmayne, Janet, and Losik in the Widener's front yard next door.

Even though the snow had stopped mid-day on Saturday, no vehicles went down highway 78 until about 4:00 p.m. on Saturday. It was a tractor heading toward Aiken, I'm sure on an errand of mercy or something very important. Otherwise, it was best to stay put, and stay safe. To say the early weather prediction missed by a mile would be an understatement.

The snowstorm completely shut down South Carolina. We had never faced snowfall of this depth and we were not prepared. Southerners don't normally have snow chains for their tires, most would not be able to even drive in these conditions, that would take experience which we did not have. "Snow storm of the century" was definitely not an understatement. Eighteen inches fell in our little community, twenty-three in some areas of Orangeburg County. A Northern winter had dropped in on Dixie.

19. A Son is Born

"A baby will make love stronger, days shorter, nights longer, bankroll smaller, home happier, clothes shabbier, the past forgotten and the future worth living for"
—unknown

My second child was due July 17, 1973. Of course, I had no clue as to the sex of this child either, but both Jimmy and Papa J.A. were hoping for a boy. I did notice that my protruding belly was lower and shaped different from when I was carrying Melanie. With Melanie, I looked like I had a basketball under my shirt and she was higher under my rib cage. Maybe this was a boy after all.

There were limitations as to what he would be named. His first name had to start with a J and his middle name had to be Allen. With those limitations in mind, we had decided if I had a boy his name would be Jason Allen. If the baby was a girl I had decided on Charlotte Kelli. It was kind of nice not to know. A surprise was always good, even though, not knowing boy or girl, you normally bought clothing and necessities in yellow and green, not pink and blue.

The baby was due on Tuesday, July 17. I had a doctor's appointment early that morning. Dr. Niles Borop, my ob/gyn doctor. Dr. Borop was a nice guy, gray hair cut in a flat top, black rimmed glasses and a fatherly bedside manner. This baby would be born at Aiken Hospital.

After the examination, Dr. Borop said, "You are ready to have this baby. Come to the hospital around two this afternoon and I'll induce labor."

"That sounds fine to me, Dr. Borop," I replied. "The only problem is my husband is in the US Army Reserve and is in Hattiesburg, Mississippi for his two-week summer training."

"That won't be a problem," he replied. "Go to the Red Cross office here in town and they will contact the necessary people and have your husband sent home. He should be here before this baby arrives, sometimes even second time mother's take their time." He then gave me a signed request to give the Red Cross personnel. After talking to the Red Cross, I went home to get my bag and called Jimmy to let him know to expect a reprieve from his summer training in Camp Shelby, Mississippi. Summer camp lasted two weeks, this was Tuesday of his second week. They had arrived by convoy the weekend before. They always left early Saturday morning from Augusta, convoyed on the interstate, spent Saturday night at Montgomery, Alabama at a Reserve center there and left early on Sunday morning for Hattiesburg. He said at the reserve center they slept on the floor or in the back of the trucks, any place they could lay their heads.

Even though I had given him a heads up, the Red Cross request had to follow the chain of command and orders had to be cut for him to come home. The Red Cross contacted the Third Army, in turn they contacted the 81st US Army Reserve Company, who contacted the Battalion they served under, and finally the 319th Company Commander, Caption Jimmy Hopkins. Captain Hopkins had Jimmy's orders cut to release him to come home. In the Army, you don't go anywhere without orders, unless it is a two-day pass. The phone at the motor pool rang, Jimmy was told to report to the Captain.

One of his fellow mechanics said, "Oh, man, what did you do, you must be in big trouble."

"Not me," Jimmy replied. "This soldier is going home, my wife's having a baby."

He reported to Company headquarters, Captain Hopkins had his orders and had found someone who agreed to drive him to the airport at New Orleans. It was a two-hour drive from Hattiesburg to New Orleans. With his orders in hand, he was allowed to fly home for free. Of course, he had to go from New Orleans to Atlanta, Georgia, then to Augusta. He hired a taxi to take him to the Carpet Factory Outlet and Leonard, his boss, let him borrow a van for the final leg of his journey. When he arrived at the Old Aiken Hospital on Richland Avenue, I was very much in hard labor.

Dr. Borop stopped in to see me when his office closed for the day. "I'll see you in the delivery room," he said. "I am leaving you in the care of two nurses. They'll call me if I am needed. You'll be fine."

By the time Jimmy arrived around 6:00pm, I was having regular labor pains. The worst pain was in my thighs, not my back. An IV was inserted in the back of my left hand and I was given something for pain by a shot in the IV along with fluids. The pains were hard and regular. About two A.M the nurses turned me on my right side and inserted something in my spine, a saddle-block they called it. Almost immediately the pain was gone and I even dozed off.

Three hours later, I was finally wheeled into the delivery room. I remember the bright lights and seeing Dr. Borop. At 5:00 A.M. July 18, 1973, Jason Allen Widener entered the world. I remember Dr. Borop lay Jason on my stomach while he cut the umbilical cord. He was grey and covered with a white, slimy substance, but he was whimpering and Dr. Borop said he was fine. The nurses cleaned him up, Dr. McManus, the pediatrician checked him out and said he was perfect. Jason weighed in at 8 lbs., 3 ¼ oz and was 20 inches long. He was a big boy compared to his older sister.

Jimmy's parents were there and everyone was pleased as punch to have a boy. He was a cute little boy with a lot of black hair. We were in the hospital until Sunday when Jimmy took us home.

Dr. Borop told me before I went home. "If I had known it was going to take you fifteen hours to have this baby, I would have never put you in labor." One of the nurses told me Dr. Borop didn't leave the hospital, he caught some shut eye on a cot waiting on me to go to the delivery room. He was there if I had any complications. Sweet man.

* * *

As far as summer camp in Hattiesburg, Jimmy didn't have to go back. The 319th left on Saturday. They, for some reason, decided to go a different way back home. Instead of spending Saturday night at a reserve center in Montgomery, Alabama, they went to Fort Benning in Columbus, Georgia. That was a decision they would regret. At Benning they had some barracks assigned to sleep in. Well, the beds in the barracks were full of bedbugs. No pun intended; the bed bugs almost ate them up. They all stripped down, most showered in an attempt to get the bedbugs off. They then went outside and slept in the trucks.

One guy climbed onto the canvas cover of a deuce and a half truck in hopes of getting some sleep. During the night the canvas split and he fell into the back of the truck. It was a miserable night for the whole company. After hearing the story, Jimmy was happy he got to come home early. He missed an awful experience on the convoy home and he had a new baby boy, Jason Allen Widener.

20 Wisdom Comes with Age

"We are all born ignorant but one must
work hard to remain stupid,"
—*Benjamin Franklin.*

"Listen to advice and accept instruction, that
you may gain wisdom in the future."
—*Proverbs 19:20 The Holy Bible*

When we are young, we tend to do stupid and sometimes very dangerous things. Young people naturally think they are immune to death. Immortal. Too young to die. They have an innate tendency to do things that older people who have been through this stage of development look at as actions to steer clear of completely.

When my husband and I were a young married couple, we did some things that were reckless and could have ended tragically. In 1975, my husband purchased a Yamaha 350 motorcycle. It was not new but, according to him it would 'scat', his terminology for 'go very fast' and believe me it did. His mother, being much older and wiser, immediately purchased a $15,000 life insurance policy on her son. She felt it was very unwise for him to be riding a motorcycle when he had a wife and two small children. We had friends, two other couples, who were into motorcycles and we often rode together on trips or just around town.

We once went to a place near Williston, called the 'grass fields' by the locals. It was basically a huge cow pasture, but the attraction was the topography, up and down rolling hills and it was so much fun to ride there. Jimmy almost threw me off the back. He said he could see my legs in his side mirrors, first on one side, then the other. I finally got off, he continued to ride up and down the grassy hills, eventually he was thrown off himself, over the handle bars. He carried bruises from this folly on his chest for weeks from the impact with the handle bars. The bruises changed colors as the healing progressed, first black, then blue, green, and finally yellow before disappearing completely. Not wise.

* * *

Jimmy had paid his uncle $125.00 to purchase a 1961 Corvair. It became my car. There was a large, oblong black mark on the back fender of the drivers' side, where a dent had been repaired with bondo. When I drove it, Melanie, our oldest child, six at the time, would duck down at traffic lights, ashamed to be seen in the car she referred to as Spot. Jimmy eventually bought a spray can of red paint from the Chevrolet dealer and painted the black mark, making it look much better. The engine was in the back of the Corvair and the trunk space in the front, like a VW beetle. Not the fanciest mode of transportation, but at least it had an engine and ran.

Once we took a memorable camping trip on land owned by the timber company, carrying all our camping equipment in the 1962 Corvair, Wayne and Cathy, our motorcycle riding friends, drove their two door Dodge Charger for the campout. We decided it was too cold to ride motorcycles. We needed room for all the gear:

tents, tools, lanterns, Coleman stove, flash lights, sleeping bags, food, and cooler. We were heading into the wilderness, far from civilization, at least as near as you can get in South Carolina. It was a tract of at least a thousand acres, without homes or people.

We camped in a great expanse of forest in the middle of nowhere. We crossed a stream, searching for a clearing among the many pines and hard woods filling this empty land. There was an old logging road to follow but no human beings for miles around, only the forest, animals that dwell in such empty spaces, and stillness. There was no traffic noise. Only the sound of birds twittering, the breeze swaying the trees, and an occasional yelp from foxes or a chirp from a squirrel surrounded us. Of course, we arrived in daylight. It was the kind of place you could easily get lost in and wander for days. We had to have daylight to find just the right spot and get the camp organized before sunset.

I had complete faith in Wayne and Jimmy, they had been on this land before hunting deer, so they knew where they were. We set up our tents, made our beds, gathered firewood, and prepared for the nighttime. We were ready when dark descended and the temperature dropped. We knew it was going to be a cold night, but we didn't expect the mercury to drop to a low of 12 degrees, thank heaven we were prepared. By sundown, we sat around the campfire, more like a bonfire, to eat our supper. Water, splashed on a bow saw brought for cutting wood, quickly froze and the solid drops could be flicked away with a thump. It was freezing.

We sat near the fire, laughing, drinking, and telling tales. We had a Coleman lantern sitting on a nearby stump and of course flashlights to find our way inside our tents. In the distance we picked up the sound of a motor heading in our direction.

Wayne said, "That must be Tommy and Pat. Tommy said they might come pay us a visit."

They rode into the firelight on Tommy's motorcycle, both wearing only light weight jackets. I knew they had to be freezing, riding a motorcycle in 12-degree weather, what were they thinking? Wisdom had no part in this night ride. They stayed a while, mostly to thaw out and warm up. The fire was blazing, but I'm sure in the back of their minds they knew they were going to have that miserable, freezing trip home. We did try to talk them into staying, even offered to take them home. They were determined to ride back, not wanting to have to return the next day for their motorcycle. I'm sure that was one ride they would remember for a long time.

Jimmy and I were prepared for the freezing weather. Inside our tent we had two sleeping bags; both could be unzipped completely to form a double-sized mat. We spread one out, put a quilt on top for our bottom layer, then we had another quilt and the other sleeping bag spread on top of that. It was a double sleeping bag that could be zipped together. We slept in our clothes, knit caps on our heads, between the quilt-lined double sleeping bag. We definitely did not get cold. The next morning, our faces were chapped from exposure to the freezing air. We had to have our faces uncovered in order to breathe. Naturally the tent was covered with frost; condensation from our breathing had coated the inside of the tent with a thin layer of ice. So much for doing sensible things, wisdom had not kicked in yet.

The next morning, with pink beginning to tint the eastern sky, just at sunrise, Jimmy crawled out of the tent. He started to stir the left-over embers of the fire from the night before, added dry wood, then green and soon had it blazing again. Wayne joined him and they put water on the Coleman stove to boil, and went to gather more wood. Cathy and I reluctantly crawled from between our warm covers and got our breakfast going. The hot water was beginning to bubble, heat rising from the pot, ready to pour over instant coffee spooned into cups. We cooked eggs and bacon in an iron skillet. By the time Wayne and Jimmy returned from their walk in the woods, with arms loaded with firewood, we were ready to eat our breakfast. It was still very cold, but the sun shone brightly and we got everything squared away before taking a hike in the woods.

It was a beautiful, crisp Winter day. Birds twittered in the trees and squirrels scurried at our passing. Our breath hung in the air like dense fog because of the cold. We were not concerned. We were warmly dressed and had nature spread before us. A canvas of brown pine straw and dried leaves covered the ground with green touches of cedar trees on a backdrop of brilliant blue above. We hiked an hour or more, never straying too far from camp, just enjoying each other's company and conversation. It was truly a peaceful, relaxing day.

Finally, we arrived at our camp, packed up our belongings, leaving the quiet solitude behind to return home, a little wiser as far as camping in freezing weather was concerned.

21. Partying at a Beach House

> "In wine there is wisdom, in beer there is
> Freedom, in water there is bacteria."
> —*Benjamin Franklin*

> "Wine is the most healthful and
> most hygienic of beverages."
> —*Louis Pasteur*

We had driven to Williston to visit our motorcycle friends, Cathy and Wayne, on a Saturday night at their house. We called it the beach house because it looked like one, not because it was at the beach. It stood on stilts, parking was underneath, and steps led up to a large, high porch and the front entrance to their house.

Melanie and Jason were staying with Papa J.A. and Super Granny Peggy, we were invited to Wayne and Cathy's, no motorcycles involved. Good thing. The weather was nice this time and we sat around their kitchen table. I don't remember what food we had, but I definitely remember the wine part. Cathy and I were drinking Mogen David grape wine, and to say we overdid the wine, an understatement. We drank five bottles between the two of us. Jimmy said he and Wayne also had wine, not as much as us girls, I'm sure. There is no one, I think, that would have five plus bottles of grape wine on their pantry shelf. Jimmy or Wayne must have made a few trips to the grocery store, I don't remember either guy leaving to purchase more. Maybe the wine fairy brought it. At the time, I probably could have been convinced of that.

Cathy and I were the only ones drinking wine, I remember. I didn't think Jimmy or Wayne were drinking any alcohol that night, but thinking back, that was highly unlikely. They were, however, aiding and abetting Cathy and myself. Whenever we finished one bottle, another magically appeared. I do remember, plates on the table, but do not remember eating any food, just drinking. When the drinking stopped, I do remember the table was sticky when I touched it with the palm of my hand.

Cathy said, "Don't worry about this sticky mess, the maid will clean it up tomorrow," referring to Wayne.

Cathy and I were laughing, joking, and having a wonderful time. Until. Wayne started frying homemade pork sausage patties. He and Jimmy were making sausage sandwiches. Must have been the aroma of the cooking and of course the excess wine drinking.

Surprise. "I think I'm going to be sick," I told Jimmy.

He led me out on the porch, one hand held his sausage sandwich, which he was gobbling, the other holding onto me as nausea hit. If he had not had a hold on me, I may have fallen over the rail. It was a good distance to the ground; I could have been seriously injured. I have always heard God takes care of drunks and fools. I guess I fit both categories on this particular night. We were saying our goodbyes, at least Wayne and Jimmy were and they were laughing. Cathy and I were laughing too, when stomach spasms and nausea didn't interfere. After the first wave passed, I was able to smile and wish them a good night's sleep. They did walk us down to the car, Cathy broke one of her clogs and cried about that; she was probably melancholy after drinking so much. Some people do get in that state, fortunately I was just nauseous. I don't think I could have survived a crying fit and being sick.

Jimmy helped me down the steep steps. No way could I have made it by myself. Thankfully there was a hand rail. He opened the passenger side and buckled my seatbelt.

Kiddingly I asked, while he was sliding under the wheel, "Want me to drive?" He gave me that have you lost your mind look and cranked the car and headed toward home.

I leaned my head against the back of the seat, he was finishing up his sausage sandwich.

"I'm going to throw up, please pull over Jimmy." I whispered with urgency. He did and I opened the door, leaned out, and puked on the side of the road. I hate to throw up, but must admit it does make me feel better.

"Are you okay?" he asked.

"I am, I just wish I had something to wipe my face."

He said, "We don't have a Kleenex. I'm sorry sweetie," Then he realized he was still holding the greasy napkin that he had wrapped around his sausage sandwich. With a shrug of his shoulders, he handed it to me, "This might help."

I took that greasy napkin and wiped my face. "That feels better," I replied, quietly and hesitantly, not realizing I had smeared that greasy sausage paper towel all over my face.

I was wearing a fake fur snap up coat Jimmy had given me as a high school graduation present. There were spots and splashes of purple and red all over my coat. I must have looked like I had been attacked by a wild animal, not wine. I got up early the next morning, even though my head felt like a punching bag and took that coat to the drycleaners. I had picked up a little wisdom that night and have never had a sip of Mogen David wine since. This was in 1975 or 1976. I have had wine since, just not Mogen David. I realize the quotes by Benjamin Franklin and Louis Pasteur may have been correct; they certainly applied to wine in moderation, not the Mogen David wine fest we two had.

22 Brush with the Law

"With age comes wisdom, but sometimes age comes alone"
— *Oscar Wilde*

"Life would be infinitely happier if we could only be born at the age of 80 and gradually approach eighteen"
— *Mark Twain*

Still doing wild and crazy stuff, even though we are in our early twenties. This story is a prime example; no wisdom involved.

We were with our motorcycle friends, visiting them in Williston as we frequently did, sharing wine (not Mogen David), crackers, and cheese. Someone suggested we go for a ride. Cathy and I sat in the back seat of our '61 Corvair with an open bottle of wine, crackers, and cheese, cut in little rectangles. The cheese and crackers would add to the enjoyment of the wine and we had packed them in sandwich bags and brought paper towels.

Jimmy or Wayne, can't remember who, suggested, "Let's ride the back roads and enjoy the cool night air." We were on Old Tory Trail, long before it was paved, definitely an unpopulated section at that time. "We'll take a spotlight and gun, do a little night hunting, maybe get a deer."

I don't remember which of the guys made the suggestion, but it did sound like a cool idea. Well, quite obviously this is against the law. Have you ever heard the phrase, 'Like a deer in the headlights?' If you shine a spotlight on deer out in an open field, they just stare and don't move. Makes it really easy to bag, all that is necessary is a fairly good marksman. Hitting a deer that stands still is 'a sitting duck' for any hunter.

Still doing stupid stuff. Geez how long does it take for young adults to develop some sense. I always thought I was fairly mature, never had a drink (except for the Mogen David, of course), smoked a cigarette, or cursed. Taught to attend church and act sensible. Now, I am about to break the law.

We all piled into the Corvair. Cathy and I in the back with refreshments. Jimmy driving, Wayne had the spotlight and a Remington semi-automatic rife with a scope, a 30-ought 6 it was called. We rode around awhile, the wine and snacks were gone, we didn't even see a deer, certainly the rifle was never fired.

On a lonely dirt road, full moon and pleasant temperatures with the front windows rolled down. Jimmy had on his old Army field jacket; Wayne may have had his on too. They were both in the same Army Reserve unit. We were so busy laughing and talking we didn't realize we were being followed, stalked is a better word. Suddenly there was a car behind us, they turned on their headlights. We had no idea we were being targeted, they had crept up behind us, no lights on until they were ready to spring their trap.

They were game wardens. Two local guys, Wardens Anderson and Wallen. We didn't know them personally. We had wandered into a trap they had set for another couple of good old boys. They knew the guilty hunters by name, but had to actually catch them in the act. They didn't catch them, they caught us. Four joy riders in the act, breaking the law, night hunting, a rifle with a scope and a spotlight. We had no defense.

One guy talked to Jimmy and Wayne, the other asked Cathy and me to put our purses on the trunk and searched them with a flashlight. Then the Warden read us our Miranda rights. "You have the right to remain silent, anything you say can and will be used against you in a court of law, you have the right to an attorney. If you cannot afford an attorney, one will be assigned to you. Do you understand these rights?" We nodded in the affirmative. Cathy and I looked at each other in bewilderment. I don't know what she was thinking, but I was thinking, *Am I dreaming, how in the hell did we go from a pleasant night ride to being arrested?* That's when they took us to jail. They handcuffed Jimmy and Wayne, separated us, the guys rode with one officer in the Corvair; Cathy and I rode with the other officer in the game warden's car. They did not handcuff Cathy and me, they knew we were already too shocked to cause any trouble. When we got to the Aiken County jail, they searched the guys. Jimmy had a pint of scotch in the field jacket pocket. Jimmy asked, "That bottle of scotch, the seal has not been broken, can I keep that?" They checked it and let him keep it. They took off the handcuffs, let us all go on our own recognizance and confiscated the car, spotlight and Wayne's rifle.

Jimmy asked, "Can we keep our baby's car seat? It's in the trunk of the Corvair." All the officers agreed that would be okay. How could they refuse, when asked such a question from a concerned Daddy? The game warden's Lieutenant was called, Mr. Jay; his brother lived up the street in Montmorenci. He took Jimmy and me home along with the car seat and dropped us off at the house. We found out there is a difference in night hunting and deer night hunting. Mr. Jay explained all this to the guys, I didn't hear any of it.

We had committed a misdemeanor, not a felony so they did let us go. Eventually Jimmy and Wayne had to go to court. The charges were dropped on Cathy and me. The guys made the front page of the Aiken Standard, top of the page 'Night Hunters plead for Mercy'. They did have to pay a fine. The car and Wayne's gun were auctioned off on the steps of the courthouse. Jimmy wanted the 61 Corvair back. He had $220.00 to bid, he was sure there would be no one to compete against, but he was wrong. The game warden who drove it to Barnwell to their impounding facility said it drove so good. He bid against Jimmy, the bidding went to $215.00, that's when his competition gave up, Jimmy won the bid with 5.00 left in his billfold. Wayne didn't bid on his rifle, I guess he just marked that up to 'lesson learned' and let it go.

We all learned a valuable lesson, but it is a story that has been told many times. I do still have the newspaper with the front-page story, of course. I have received a few speeding tickets in the years since, but no more Miranda declarations or handcuffs.

23. Camping in the Smokies.

In the early Spring of 1976, we had a big camping trip planned to the Smokie Mountains. Cathy and Wayne lived in Aiken at Greenbrier Apartments, right off Two Knotch Road, bordering today's Odell Weeks Facility and the tennis courts. They had two couples that wanted to go with us Rocky, and Dave and their significant others. Tommy and Pat went, Cathy, Wayne, Jimmy and me. Dave drove a van, Rocky was on his Harley Davidson Sportster, Tommy rode his Honda 750 motorcycle and Wayne was on his blue Honda 550 super sport with safety bar attached to the sides. They all wore helmets. I believe back then it was required. In South Carolina, now, no motorcycle rider is required to wear a helmet. Makes no sense to me, but my tale deals with the helmet question in a very personal way.

We caravanned to the mountains. Dave drove the van, leading the way. Some of the girls rode in the van along with the necessary equipment: tents, stove, lanterns, and a big cooler full of beer, probably other groceries. The guys riding motorcycles were in a v formation behind the van. Jimmy and I brought up the rear in our 72 green Vega hatchback.

Jimmy and Wayne each brought a case of C rations as our foodstuff contributions. At that time in South Carolina, you only had to be eighteen to purchase alcohol. It is no longer that way, but this was during the Vietnam war. I've always been of the opinion, if you can be drafted in the military, carry an M16 and shoot the enemy, you ought to be considered old enough to purchase alcohol. I'm sure we had plenty of beer, quite possibly some stronger spirits.

In a box of C rations there are twelve separate meals. Each of the twelve boxes contained some kind of canned meat, spaghetti and meat balls, spam, Vienna sausage etc., real good stuff, at least the spaghetti Jimmy praised. There was also cheese, crackers, chocolate brownies, a pack of four cigarettes, matches, salt and pepper packs, instant coffee, toilet paper, sugar, creamer, and a plastic spoon. Soldiers were supplied with C rations in the field. That was what we had. Jimmy still has a case of C rations in our utility room. The box is stamped 1968.

When we got to the camp site, we set up the two-man tents, some slept in sleeping bags in Dave's van. Early April in the smokies, the weather is still chilly, plants and trees are just beginning to put forth leaves and it was nice to sit around a blazing fire that first night. Jimmy remembers cutting thin branches, stripping the leaves and buds to use for toasting marshmallows around the fire and cooking hot dogs.

The next day we decided to hike up Mount Le Conte, one of the highest mountains in the Appalachian chain, 5,301 feet from the base. It reaches skyward near Gatlinburg, Tennessee and is totally within the National park. The hiking trail we took up the mountain was steep. Little animals scurried out of our way and the sun was hot where the shade receded from the dirt path. I was so ready to turn around and go down. Once we reached the top, the trail became strenuous and I was afraid to pass anyone. It was a long way down and my calves and thighs were sore from the pull up the winding, rocky, and narrow dirt path. I did sit down to catch my breath, we all did. It was a beautiful vista from the rock outcroppings that we used as seats, but I dreaded the trip back down. I knew it would be easier than the climb up, but it would be treacherous. We were all tired, I'm sure. We rested a while, just enjoying the view from the top.

Finally, we determined we had better head back to camp. It would take a while and we wanted to be back at camp before darkness enveloped the mountain. My limbs ached and it would be so easy to make a misstep and slip over the edge. I went down slowly and tried to be aware of where I put my feet, a loose stone or a vine crossing the path could cause a fall.

We reached more level ground, the path slowly became less treacherous, I was more at ease mentally, but my legs still ached. Finally, I could see the narrow bridge crossing the swift stream we had traversed on our trek up to the summit. Beyond that was our campsite.

* * *

Saturday night, lots of fun around the campfire. It was chilly in the mountains in early April. A few folding chairs, and old blankets spread on the ground. Even a couple of short logs too big for the fire. We were young then and had no trouble getting up off the ground. We mostly sat Indian style, the way I did when I was a kid. Of course, we had plenty of beer and coolers. I was not a beer drinker at that time, mostly wine coolers for me. All the guys were puffing on cigarettes, maybe something else. If so, I was not aware, but we were the hippie generation. I started smoking cigarettes much later, in my thirties. There was music and laughter, a transistor radio blasting Kasey Kasem's countdown.

Sunday morning dawned cool and crisp. The guys built a fire, and we ate some more C rations before breaking camp. We wanted it to warm up a bit, at least the motorcycle riders did. Around noon, we were finally ready to pack up and go home. Dave in the lead in the van with the ladies, the v shape motorcycle group, only guys. Two in front then the third, Wayne on his Honda. Jimmy and I brought up the rear in the Vega.

We finally got to Edgefield, almost home. Somewhere along the way, Jimmy and I had traded places, riding on Wayne's Honda. Wayne and Cathy were now in our Vega with Wayne behind the wheel, bringing up the rear. We took the bypass around Edgefield, it was dark and since it was still chilly, Jimmy was wearing Wayne's leather jacket, we both were wearing helmets and I had on long sleeves.

This is a testament to the fact; it takes only seconds to change your life. A car was about to pass, heading in the opposite direction. At the time, I saw the car in the other lane, I remember feeling the up and over like a speed bump. It was a dog. A German Sheppard walked into the highway in front of us and behind the first two motorcycles. Jimmy had to make a split-second decision. He could take the ditch, the other lane in front of the speeding car, or hit the dog. He chose the dog. As soon as we cleared the dog, the cycle fell over on the left side and skidded down the other side of the roadway. It felt like a sling-shot had flung the motorcycle down the opposite lane. It could not have lasted more than five seconds. The metal safety bar kept our legs off the highway, there were sparks filling the night air, jumping all around. I could literally feel my head bouncing off the pavement. Needless to say, the helmet saved my life.

Jimmy jumped up and righted the motorcycle, getting it off the highway. The dog was convulsing as he lay in the ditch dying. Everyone stopped, the guy who had just passed turned around and came back to see if we were okay. The hand clutch on the motorcycle was broken, the forearm of Wayne's leather jacket was skinned and the helmet I was wearing was badly scratched from contact with the pavement. Wayne got on his motorcycle, the other guys rigged up a tow, decided that wasn't going to work. The others went on ahead. We definitely didn't want to report the accident to the law as long as everyone was okay.

Jimmy, Cathy, and I were back in the Vega following Wayne on his motorcycle. Jimmy was driving, Cathy was in the back, and I sat in the front. My teeth were chattering, I couldn't stop trembling. Thinking maybe I could go into shock; Cathy gave me a pill. I have no idea what I took, something to help me calm down. I did begin to relax as we slowly continued on our journey back to Greenbriar Apartments. Because of the broken clutch, we had to follow Wayne at a slow pace.

I kept thinking what could have happened. If the car that passed had been even five seconds earlier, he would have hit us. Both Jimmy and I could well have been killed. After that accident, I rode that motorcycle with Jimmy only once more.

* * *

That concludes our biggest adventures with Wayne and Cathy. We are still friends but see them seldom. They divorced, Cathy remarried, Wayne stayed single. They visited us often and we visited them, Jimmy served with Wayne in the Army Reserve until 1976. They rode together to weekend meetings and had summer camps together. Those summer camps in Hattiesburg, Mississippi would produce a wealth of entertaining stories. I have heard a few from Jimmy. We eventually drifted apart, but stay in touch. Life is certainly like a revolving door, friends and acquaintances go around entering and exiting our lives, sometimes at a dizzying speed. My story would not be complete without our seventy's adventures with them.

24. Back to the Past

*"If history were taught in the form of
stories, it would never be forgotten"*
— Rudyard Kipling

If you want to understand today, you
have to search yesterday
— Pearl Buck

In the early 1970's, I developed a great interest in genealogy, the research and recording of my ancestry. I attribute the almost fanatical hobby that developed to several things: the stories told by family members, especially my Uncle Leon, Daddy, and my Grandma Florence, and to interaction with Aunt Jennie Gantt Rish, tidbits of information that could be verified. I had often visited my Aunt Jennie, sister to my Granddaddy Kelly Gantt. Aunt Jennie lived until 1985, I knew her well. She told stories about her parents, Kel and Peninnah Woodward Gantt. She also showed me the large ornate framed photograph of Ara Gunter Woodward, mother of Peninnah, my great grandmother. As I gazed on Ara's countenance, the plain features, an expression of a hard-working woman, no frills and lots of wrinkles. She appeared to be dressed in a blouse with lace around the neckline, hair pulled tight in a bun, I pondered to myself, *this face is my great, great grandmother who died in 1864. What must her life have been like then?* I had always been fascinated by history, the why and how events take place. Now I just wanted to know my ancestors and what it was like in their lifetime.

I was always, at least from an early age, aware that all human beings are mortal and I didn't want their memories to completely disappear. Every human being has a story and I wanted to tell mine and my families' while there was still time. I wanted to leave something behind, something that generations would be able to relate to. My life is only a small wrinkle in time, a hiccup in the grand scheme of time. As stated in the Bible, 'For what is your life? It is even a vapour that appeareth for a little time, and then vanisheth away.' (James 4:14) The Holy Bible

Recently among my family papers, legal documents, letters, death and birth records, I found a letter Aunt Jennie had written to her niece in Atlanta, Cleola Gantt Woodward. The names, birth and death dates of Jennie's grandparents, Ulysses S. and Martha Matilda Cook Gantt and her great grandparents Elijah and Elizabeth Gunter Gantt were recorded.

Surprisingly, I found, especially in the 70's and 80's, many people, family, and friends had no interest whatsoever in their ancestry. Some did not even know the identity of their grandparents, much less, further back in their line of descent.

I began research long before the internet and ancestry.com. I visited cemeteries, court houses, archives, and interviewed all older family members. Some of the folks I interviewed back then also shared their stories, memories, and in many cases old photos of family relations. I joined the Lexington County Genealogical Society, where I got referrals to people who were researching some of the same family surnames. These people I often wrote to and I started receiving correspondence in the form of letters from all over the U.S. Hard to believe, very few people even write letters now. The present generation is not even taught the correct form of letters. They depend completely on text messages, emails, or social media. I don't mean to downplay the importance of these forms of communication. I, myself, have an iPhone, not that I know how to use all the features, but it is convenient. I do, however, mourn the loss of cursive writing. It is not taught in public schools any longer. I can't comprehend how a signature, especially on legal documents, can be your name printed. I guess cursive really will be the secret code for the older generation.

In 1977, along came the mini-series, Roots, and suddenly people, black and white, wanted to know where they were from and stories that connected their family. Alex Haley had written a phenomenal book about his family and stories told sitting on the front porch at his boyhood home of Henning, Tennessee. I thought the book was amazing.

Most of the stories I heard from my family during my childhood were told in the evenings, sitting on the porch. Season did not matter, even in the muggy nights of August or the freezing temperatures of January. It was a wonderful setting in the dark of night, no security lights to interfere, actually, no porch lights on during warm weather to discourage pesky insects. The front porch was always a good place to sit and talk. The house was not cool in August nor warm and snug in January, so the porch was generally a good alternative for conversation. Spring and early Fall it was truly nice. A cool breeze swaying the trees across the dirt road, night birds calling, and a heaven full of stars. That was a childhood.

Back to my need to research. I have many spiral, lined

Kathy Widener

notebooks with notes from interviews with relatives. Most have names, dates, and tidbits of information from those that are no longer with us. I ask only to preserve their voices and stories with the written word.

25. Events to be Remembered

> History is not "a burden on the memory
> but an illumination of the soul"
> —*Lord Acton*

There will always be historical events that stand out in the mind of every person. The question for humanity is, do we remember these important events? If they are bad, will we learn from them? There are historical events that stand out in my memory and I find that I can remember, in most cases, when they happened and where I was when they took place.

The first memory that was really a major moment for our country was the launching of the first orbiting satellite, Sputnik 1 by the Russians. It began America's space race. Sputnik 1 orbited the earth from October, 1957 until January, 1958 when its orbit deteriorated. It burned up reentering the earth's atmosphere. We kids would go out on the north porch, sit on the top wooden step in the darkness, and wait for that little pinpoint of light moving from west to east in the night sky. Because we lived in the country, away from city lights, we had no outside lighting, only one bulb in the center of the porch ceiling. We pulled the string to cut off that meager light, so we could find Sputnik easier. There was complete blackness all around us as we huddled together, my siblings and I in the darkness and cold, breath hanging in the night air. It didn't take long to spot the tiny bright object in the sky among the millions of stars, simply because it was the only one moving. The bright orb of the moon was not present, only a canopy of millions of stars in the night sky. The space race with Russia was on. America had to outpace our Cold War enemies.

* * *

In 1960, I recall watching the first presidential debate on television. It was in black and white, not color. Being only nine, I didn't have any interest in politics, but I did think John F. Kennedy was better looking than Richard Nixon. As it turned out, Kennedy became a household name after the debate. Before, according to the news, a lot of people had no idea who he was or what he looked like. Television helped John F. Kennedy win the presidency that November. I guess it's hard to gauge the stature of a man from hearing only a disembodied voice coming from a radio. With so many Americans having a relatively new technology, television sets, in their homes, it turned out to be the determining factor.

President Kennedy was very supportive of America winning the space race against the Russians. America did not send the first man into space, that was a Russian, Yuri Gagarin, in April 1961, but after Russia's success. America's space program took off, no pun intended. Alan Sheppard made a suborbital flight barely a month after Gagarin in May 1961.

On February 20, 1962, when I was in fifth grade, John Glenn rocketed into history, aboard the Friendship 7. We fifth graders heard Walter Cronkite, a favorite respected newsman, describe and narrate Commander Glenn's progress over the PA system at school. The radio broadcast from the office reached Miss Hook's fifth grade via a brown wooden box high on the classroom wall. We didn't get non-stop coverage, but every so often, Mrs. Smith, the school secretary, interrupted class with an update. This was a big deal. It was important that America's children actually hear this historical event.

* * *

On November 22, 1963, I walked from Miss Powell's literature class at the back of Pelion school, entered the door of the library wing for my study hall in the library. It was around 1:30 P.M. on a Friday afternoon. The librarian, Mrs. Nichols, was speaking from the office over the PA system. President John F. Kennedy had been assassinated in Dallas, Texas. The devastating news was being announced by Walter Cronkite as I entered the library. My fellow students and I listened to the news through the public address system the remainder of that day. As we listened, I only remember the feeling of shock and dread that permeated every space in the school. When the final bell rang, students headed quietly for the school buses, no jostling, laughter, or running in the halls. It was like walking through a thick cloud, lost, unable to see. Despair and uncertainty settled all around us. For the first time in my young life, a tragic event affected all Americans, our President had been assassinated. I had never experienced grief, never lost a close family member, but this event was somber sorrow for all ages of Americans united in grief.

When we got home, it was non-stop news coverage on our television; the capture of assassin, Lee Harvey Oswald outside a movie theater, video of President Kennedy's limo at Dealey Plaza, the sound of loud pops, our President slumped over in the back seat, and the speeding up of the limo taking him to Parkland Hospital.

Then, the still photo of Vice President Lyndon B. Johnson being sworn in by a lady judge on Air Force One. Mrs. Kennedy stood beside him in a daze, still in her blood-stained suit. The images were heartbreaking. I can only imagine how dramatic and horrific the images would have been in color; we only had a black and white television at the time. That evening Air Force One landed at Andrews Air Base near Washington and the president's coffin was off loaded and placed in a waiting hearse. Even at this late hour, we were still glued to the television.

    The next three days there was non-stop news reporting. The president's coffin was reverently carried up the steps of the Capitol on Sunday by a military honor guard. He lay in state in the rotunda as thousands of Americans passed by quietly to pay their respects to our fallen president. The news reported that some waited in line for five hours.

* * *

Out in Dallas, Texas, Lee Harvey Oswald was being moved to a different facility. He was flanked by law enforcement, men in suits wearing fedora hats. Oswald had on a dark pullover sweater, handcuffed and being pushed through the crowd of reporters and photographers. A pistol appeared in the bottom corner of the screen. Suddenly, Jack Ruby shot Oswald, killing him on live television before law enforcement could prevent his murder.

* * *

I watched the presidential funeral on Monday, November 25th at Grandma's brother, Eugene and his wife, Aunt Ethel's house. They were living in Wagener at the time. I can remember sitting cross-legged on the floor in front of the television and watching the procession. The President's coffin, covered with the Stars and Stripes, was strapped in an open caisson. Following the casket was a riderless black horse; black boots were attached to the stirrups in a backward position as the horse was led by a soldier. I remember thinking how wild eyed that horse appeared. Thousands upon thousands of people lined the funeral route to Arlington National Cemetery where the President was interred. An eternal flame would be lit in front of the modest white marble head stone.

The whole country mourned President John F. Kennedy, he was only forty-six years old. It was an emotional event, shocking, sad, and devastating for all Americans.

* * *

Even after his death, President Kennedy's dream of sending astronauts into space continued, culminating in the landing of Neil Armstrong and Buzz Aldrin on the moon, July 20, 1969. My husband and I had been married less than a month when America's crowning achievement occurred. We went out to supper that evening in Augusta, Georgia and stopped by to visit Jimmy's cousin, Jane and her husband in North Augusta. We watched the moon landing there. It was so exciting when we heard the words, "The Eagle has landed."

Neil Armstrong came down the short ladder, stepping onto the actual powdery surface of the moon, and uttered those famous words, "One small step for man, one giant leap for Mankind."

Other astronauts would follow, but Apollo 11 and those first steps were the pinnacle for the space program. To think, their footprints are still there and the American flag they planted, not fluttering, because of zero gravity, but still and proud as if America had staked claim to the moon.

* * *

In June 1993, I went to work for the business office at Aiken Regional Medical Centers. I was working at my desk on the fateful morning of September 11, 2001. I remember a lady, Linda, rushed out of the file room and reported that a commercial airplane, a Boeing 757, hit one of the twin towers of the World Trade Center in New York City. When a second airliner hit the other tower minutes later, it was obvious this was a planned attack. Linda, our informant, was frantic, as were all of us, but Linda's sister worked at the Trade Center. She was finally able to contact her at home. The sister had called in sick, Devine providence, I would say. A television was set up in one of the classrooms down the hall and we were told by our supervisor that we could go and watch.

New York City was in chaos. People were trying to escape the fires and explosions caused as the planes crashed into both buildings. Each of the buildings were 110 floors tall, so people on the upper floors were doomed. Firemen and police entered the buildings to help survivors escape. The only way out for many were the stairwells opposite from the conflagrations where the planes penetrated. There were reports of people in the upper floors phoning their loved ones to say goodbye and the desperate, knowing there was no escape, jumping from windows. Many were seen taking their own lives, hurling their bodies from the upper floors to their deaths. Awful tragic scenes, seared into the memories of New Yorkers and all Americans.

The unthinkable happened two hours after the initial hits, the towers completely collapsed, 2,606 people were killed plus 150 onboard the two hijacked aircraft. Watching those buildings pancake down and the massive dust and debris bellowing out in every direction was horrific. These planes had been taken by terrorists from Logan Airport in Boston; the plan was the mastermind of Arab terrorists. Two other planes were highjacked that day, one hit the Pentagon in Washington D.C. and the other, crashed in the countryside of Pennsylvania. Brave passengers took back the plane from the terrorists, but all were killed in the crash.

News coverage from New York City, showed a city filled with distraught people wandering the streets in a daze, posting pictures of their loved ones on bulletins boards, hoping against all odds that they had escaped and someone might recognize them from the posted photographs. It would be many months before any remains could be identified, most never.

We had experienced a terrorist attack on American soil, many good people died that day. A day that no American should ever forget.

* * *

In the Spring of 1989, I interviewed an old gentleman, Seldon Gantt who lived at that time in Batesburg, SC. I recently rediscovered the notes from that visit with Mr. Seldon and his amazing story. Mr. Seldon was born in 1911, so when I had the great fortune to interview him, he was seventy-eight years old. I arranged to meet the old gentleman to question him about his memories of my great, great grandfather, James Andrew Caughman. Mr. Selman was a first cousin to my Grandpa, Coley Hartley. Both Seldon and Grandpa were grandsons of James A. Caughman, born in 1849, died in December 1938. Mr. Seldon told me what he could remember about Grandpa Caughman, who was called "one-eyed

Jim". According to Mr. Seldon, Grandpa Caughman, reaching on the mantle, knocked a pair of scissors down; the sharp point of the scissors stabbed his eye and destroyed his sight in that eye.

Mr. Seldon told several interesting stories about Grandpa Caughman, from his eye witness knowledge. Grandpa 'one-eyed' Jim claimed to be a horse trader, always dressed in black and wore a white shirt. According to Mr. Gantt, Grandpa outlived his wife by a good many years. His wife was Sallie Swygert. Jim and Sallie lived just seven miles from Aiken on #1 highway. Grandma Sallie died as a result of a boil on her spine that became horribly infected. From his description, Grandma Caughman suffered with terrible pain and infection that seeped from the boil continuously. Seldon was seventeen at the time and could remember her quite well. He also had first-hand knowledge of the character of Grandpa Jim. He was very forthcoming as far as Grandpa Caughman was concerned. According to Mr. Seldon, Grandpa considered his vocation a horse trader, but could be described as a nere-do well, in other words, he didn't like to work. He referred to a time when Grandpa Jim had a visitor on a Sunday, Wade Miles, who spent the night with the Caughmans. Mr. Miles brought with him about ten old horses. He and Grandpa Jim rounded them up on Monday to take them to a horse sale in Aiken. The two ended up spending a week in Aiken drinking liquor. They must have sold the horses and had a high old time with the proceeds. It was very interesting to speak to someone who had known my great, great grandparents and was willing to speak candidly about them.

It turned out that Mr. Seldon had a much more amazing story to tell. Grandpa Caughman was a Confederate Soldier who enlisted in Company D, 20th Regiment on the 16th day of October 1864 and fought until April 1865. Grandpa was only fifteen years old when he joined. Mr. Seldon had first-hand information about

Every Life Tells a Story

an historical event of great significance, it didn't take place in my lifetime. But I interviewed a witness who was there. I believe it is well worth including.

From June 27 to July 5, 1938, the 75th Reunion of Civil War Veterans was held at Gettysburg, PA. It would be the final reunion for the blue and gray. This group of veterans was almost all of those remaining alive. Gettysburg was selected as the most desirable site for a final reunion as it contributed more than any battle to the losses on both sides.

The Federal Government paid all expenses for the frail old veterans from all across the United States to attend, along with one attendant for each. Mr. Seldon attended this final reunion with Grandpa Caughman. He was an eyewitness to this very important historical event. Sitting there as he told this story, I'm sure I was somewhat wide-eyed knowing I was actually face to face with someone who could give a first-hand account of the goings on at Gettysburg so long ago. The government spared no expense, big tents with comfortable accommodations were set up, even had wooden floors in the tents. There were medical facilities, food preparation and serving, and even a place for the old gentlemen to congregate, have a drink of liquor, and discuss their memories of the War.

I happened to have in my possession a copy of the Military Medical Report 75th Reunion of the Battle of Gettysburg authored by Earl C. Lowery MD, Colonel Medical Corp USA. It is absolutely fascinating.

The following is from the report authored by Dr. Lowery. "My instructions from the Surgeon General USA were: (1) to furnish medical care for the unit to which I was attached, (2) to hold sick call for the Civil War Veterans attending the reunion, both Blue and Gray, (3) to furnish needed medical care for President Franklin D. Roosevelt who was the guest speaker July 4, 1938.

"The Secretary of War and his staff had carefully planned the reunion. They had detailed plans for medical coverage for the 2,000 veterans of both sides of the War expected to attend. This reunion would be the last one – a joint one for Union and Confederate. Approximately 2,000 signed up to come: 1,980 came. The youngest one I saw was ninety-one and the oldest 116," stated Dr. Lowery.

"These 1,980 veterans offered a rare opportunity for clinical observation, both Medical and Military. The average height was 5 feet 8 inches, average weight was 145. They wore beautiful suits: 80% wore suspenders, few belts, always loose. They appeared well, erect, rare canes and few crutches.

"At certain parts of the programs a few veterans, both Blue and Gray, wore uniform coats and medals. Several scuffles occurred when veterans so dressed got into discussions and arguments. There were no fat men. Few had hearing aids. It was an energetic group.

"The eyes of the veterans, all above ninety, presented rare clinical soundness. Many did not have glasses. I inquired of one veteran at sick call (who was getting whiskey) and he replied, "I can see everything around here close and I don't care what's out yonder."

"We scheduled sick call at 6:00 a.m. The first man in a long line, a Mr. Heflin from Texas, said, "I've been here since 4:00 a.m. Where have you been? Hand me my bottle." (Free whiskey was available). He wanted no medical attention. We moved sick call up to 5:00 a.m. for obvious reasons. The following day at 4:45 a.m. Mr. Heflin was first in line and asked for a bottle. After inquiring about yesterday's bottle and recommendations on dosage, he stated that yesterday's bottle was consumed by him alone and that he must have another. When advised this might be an overdose, he replied, "In 1848, I went from Heflin, Alabama to Texas. In route

Every Life Tells a Story

I came down with typhoid fever. I went downhill for seven weeks to almost death. The Doctor said, "put him on whiskey and let him die comfortably." They did and I got well. I have had my bottle every day since. Don't you think I am a bit old to quit?"

"How old are you?" I asked.

"I am one hundred and seven." I gave him his bottle.

"One highlight of the reunion was an address by the President of the United States, Franklin D. Roosevelt.

"When Mr. Roosevelt gave his speech dedicating the Peace Memorial, Mr. Seldon told me. "Grandpa Caughman and myself were standing near the President when he lit the torch for the eternal flame."

Dr. Lowery said, "I watched a group, about eight, showing how and where they fought in Pickett's Charge. They actually ran, jumped a ditch and fence, then ran up a hill. One veteran broke his leg at the fence. While helping him back he stated that when he jumped the ditch in battle it was full of blood and wider. When asked how much water was in the ditch, he said, "None, it was waist deep in blood."

"A graves registration Company of the First Medical Regiment was detailed to carry out mortuary mission at the reunion. They had consulted six major insurance companies. The question, how many deaths would occur in bringing 2,000 veterans to this reunion for five days from all over the United States, average age 100?

"After much study and careful analysis of the reports of consultants, it was concluded there would be sixty-six deaths, there were two deaths, one en-route home.

"I'll never forget the look on the unit commander's face when he said, "There are three kinds of lies: lies, damned lies, and statistics."

Kathy Widener

This obviously was not a historical event that took place in my lifetime, but the eye witness interview did. When I think that I actually sat with Mr. Seldon Gantt, a man who was present for the last Civil War Reunion, I am absolutely amazed. I just wish I had asked more questions about that last reunion.

26. Teaching by Example

"Train up a child in the way he should go: and when he is old, he will not depart from it."
—*Proverbs 22:6 The Holy Bible*

In 1975, Jason was just a toddler, with chubby cheeks and fat folds on his legs like the Michelin Tire man. Jimmy was still selling carpet in Augusta and driving all over Aiken County and down a lonely highway in South Georgia. He called this South Georgia trek, the woodpecker trail. It was a lot of empty land, sprinkled with small towns and bumpy crossroads along railroad tracks. He was measuring and selling carpet to make ends meet, no matter how far he had to go. Many nights he came home in the wee hours, I waited up, sometimes perched on the humpback of Grandma's old trunk. Her daddy had bought it for her belongings when they had been uprooted to upstate, Marlboro County, in the 1890's. Grandma had given it to me before she died. The trunk sat in my paneled, red shag carpeted den right in front of the window. I would sit there on that metal trunk with grape vines in relief decorating the outside, leather strips on each end to heist it aboard the train, waiting to see lights beaming from the Vega as Jimmy turned onto Woodward Drive.

Sometimes, Melanie, Jason, and I would go with him in the

late afternoon if a carpet job was close and he would be passing our house. Once we went to Williston with him to measure for carpet. The owners had a son a little older than Jason. The children were playing in the little boy's room when sounds of a fuss reached my ears.

Excusing myself, I said, "I'll go check on the children, see if Melanie and Jason are behaving, be right back."

When I entered the room, Melanie stood in front of Jason holding him back with both hands, arms extended behind her like open shears. She was protecting him from the other boy. She looked like a coon dog staring down a ring tail. From the day I brought him home, she always tried to help me take care of him. The other kid was banishing a plastic knife, like a swashbuckling pirate swooping the air in their direction, making ever threatening growling noises.

"He was going to stick my little brother, Momma," she said, glancing up at me. "I wasn't going to let him do that."

I gently took Jason by the hand, Melanie trailing behind and we retreated back to the den. Jimmy had finished his measuring calculations and we left. I told Melanie I was proud that she was taking up for her little brother and protecting him. I didn't say it was just a plastic knife and he was just a little kid, I wanted her to know she was doing the right thing.

* * *

When Jason was three years old, he and I went to the drug store, Eckerd's on the south side of Aiken. Melanie was in kindergarten at East Aiken Elementary. He disappeared from my site and I began to look for him. There was a hose display, it was tall, round like a carousel with dozens of panty hose tucked inside what looked like large plastic eggs. It was a Leggs display, each egg held a pair of hose. Jason was behind the display purposely hiding from me. When I found him, he had a large snickers candy bar, open and half eaten. He knew he was doing something wrong. The chocolate smeared on his little face would have given him away even if I hadn't caught him red-handed. I took the candy from his chocolate pudgy hand and led him towards the front of the store, lecturing him all the way about how wrong it was to steal something that was not yours. He didn't protest, he knew he was in trouble. I placed the half-eaten bar on the counter.

"My son has something to say to you," I told the man standing at the register.

The guy peered over the counter to look directly into the upturned little boy's face, shame written all over his expression.

"How can I help you buddy?" he asked.

Jason replied in a quiet voice, "I took this candy bar, mister, without paying, I sure am sorry."

I paid for the candy bar, handed it to Jason. Beside the glass exit doors stood a metal trash can. "Throw the snickers in the trash son."

When we got home, Jason got the spanking he so richly deserved. We did not have timeout at our house. I explained why, reiterating, how wrong it was to take something that does not belong to you. "Let this be a lesson to you, son, don't do that again."

***

When Melanie went to kindergarten, she attended the second session every day. A school bus picked her up at 11:00 and brought her home after 2:00. I still remember the day she started. She wore a red checked dress with a white bodice embroidered with a bunch of flowers. Jason and I would sit on the front porch to see she got on the bus okay and waited for her to get home in the afternoon.

One afternoon when she was dropped off, she climbed the embankment from the road bent over and put something on the ground behind one of the Oaks in the front yard. As she started up the front steps I asked, "What did you put on the ground behind the tree?"

"Nothing, Momma," was her reply.

"Well, let's go see what that nothing is."

On the ground was a folded piece of notebook paper. It was a note from her teacher about her talking in class and not paying attention to the teacher. We had a discussion about the misbehavior, but the bigger offense was lying when I asked her. She didn't get a spanking, only a good talking to about telling the truth. Avoiding trouble at all cost is an instinct ever child is born with. I was only striving to let Melanie know, honesty is very important, always.

* * *

When Jason was about four years old, he was playing around at his Papa J.A. and Granny Peggy's. His Papa J.A. worked for the City of Aiken, Assistant Superintendent of Streets and Parks. He drove a blue city truck home from work every day. Somehow, Jason got into the cab of the city truck. The passenger window was rolled down, maybe four inches, and Jason had his foot stuck in that opening. He was sprawled on the seat, leg in the air and foot wedged. He called and called for his Granny, to no avail. She was inside cooking supper and didn't hear him. Finally, his Aunt Charmayne, walking to their house, heard his yelling for his Grandma and rescued him from his Papa's truck. She chewed him out, but good, for getting in the truck and told him to stay out of vehicles.

He told his Granny Peggy, "I called and called for you, but you didn't come. I prayed God would help me."

"Well son, God did help you. He did send Aunt Charmayne to help you."

Surely, thinking about the dressing down he had just received from Aunt Charmayne, Jason replied, "Looks like he could have sent you."

* * *

When Jason began to take care of his bathroom needs himself, bathing without splashing too much water on the carpet, getting out of the tub and drying off and of course potty care, he considered himself a 'big boy'. I was proud of his progress. He was four years old and I was expecting another baby. I appreciated only having to check on him, knowing he was capable of taking care of his own hygiene.

One afternoon, I was walking down the hall, glancing into the bathroom as I passed. Jason was perched on the baby blue commode with his pants down, his feet dangling. "You need any help, son?"

"No, Momma, I can take care of it."

"I know you can, you're not a baby anymore."

He began to unravel half of the toilet tissue roll in his small hands. Noticing the big wads of tissue, he was using, I made a suggestion.

"Don't use so much tissue when you clean your bottom." I showed him, children need to see to understand. "Use six sheets to begin," measuring them so he could remember. "You can always get more, if needed."

"Okay, I will," was his reply.

Two weeks later, I was in the kitchen cooking supper when Jason starting calling, "Momma," from the bathroom.

"Jimmy, please go see what Jason wants, I can't leave the stove right now."

Returning five minutes later, Jimmy said with a confused look, "I don't know what in the world he was talking about, Jason said, tell Momma I accidently used seven sheets."

I couldn't help but laugh knowing my four-year-old son had been dutifully counting out six sheets of tissue at the time for the last two weeks.

I was aiming for a lesson in not being wasteful, but just goes to show, innocent young children tend to take adults literally.

27. Then Along Came Baby

In late Spring 1977, I got the news from Dr. Bruns in Augusta that I was expecting. This baby would be born at the University Hospital in Augusta, Georgia. Dr. Borop, who delivered Jason, had retired; Dr. Bruns was recommended by a friend.

That summer in July, Jimmy, Melanie, Jason, and I took a camping trip to Edisto Beach. The heat was absolutely crushing and I was pregnant and miserable. I lay on the padded floor of our two-man tent. A box fan vibrated on the end of a long extension cord blowing directly on me. Even with the fan blades whirling on high, the heat index could not be defeated. The fan was spinning out only super-heated air, no relief.

When evening came, we walked on the beach. Frothy foam crawled over my feet, tickling my toes. The water felt so cool and refreshing. I begin to feel a bit of relief. The sun, a blazing fire ball of orange, descending on the horizon. The churning surf coupled with the setting sun stirred a slight cool breeze. I felt hopeful that at least the night would be better with a cool respite of wind; the sound of the pounding surf, a calming noise. I felt the quickening of the child I was carrying and smiled dozing off to sleep, dreaming of home and air-conditioning.

Kathy Widener

* * *

Dr. Bruns said my pregnancy was going fine. I got to hear my baby's heartbeat, an incredibly fast … bump, bump, bump… as he positioned the stethoscope over my growing belly. Cool breezes and falling leaves elevated my mood as the heat of summer retreated; Melanie and Jason were so excited for their little baby brother or sister to arrive. We wouldn't know until delivery. This baby would be Jared Micah or Lori Paige, none of us were concerned about the sex of our new baby. It did not matter what I had.

Our baby was due in January 1978. Jimmy had just started a new job at the Savannah River Site working in the Service Department cleaning floors and emptying trash cans. He was working 2nd shift, 4pm to midnight the first eight weeks. Then would attend a production class for reactor training, eventually becoming a Reactor Operator in P Area, working swing shift.

December and January were extremely cold months. The temperature plummeted into the teens at night throughout the entire month of January. The wind's breath stifled my own as I tromped out to the clothesline to hang up the wash. My big belly was a detriment when a task required bending and lifting. I had to be extra careful carrying the wicker basket down the side steps as chilling winds swayed treetops and blew my hair, plastering it to my face at every turn. Once I reached the clothesline, dropping my burden, I dipped into the woven wicker basket, picked up one piece of clothing at a time. Giving each a good shake, I dug wooden clothes pegs from a cloth bag attached to a hanger and pinned each piece to the line.

The children were safer inside, wrapped in a blanket in front of the den TV. When night descended and the temperature started to fall, we closed off the den and the heat vents in there to help minimize our heating oil bill. We had no electric dryer. As you can imagine, Jimmy's new job as a janitor did not pay a lot. He would arrive from work after midnight, head straight through the den and close the door behind him. Melanie and Jason were already tucked in bed, I waited for him, propped up in bed, usually reading. I didn't watch TV, the den needed to be closed off and there were few channels to watch, WJBF, WRDW both from Augusta, sometimes we could pick up WIS in Columbia. Now it was in color, but still, not the obsession of today, with unlimited channels.

It reminded me of my childhood when winter time was spent only in the kitchen, the whole family together. We experienced that same togetherness that January of 1978, closing off the den and the folding doors to the left of our front foyer. We had a living room behind the folding doors, seldom used. The shag carpet was white, the furniture was a gold velvet sectional sofa we had purchased from an ad in the Carolina Trader. There was a lamp table between the sections and a gold chair and ottoman. It was made in the Spanish style, even with a round bowl, black wrought iron, that nestled in a perfectly made-to-fit hole in the table. There were two iron implements that came with this bowl. They served no purpose, just decoration. How did we really determine the Spanish intended influence? Included was a large gold and black framed picture of a matador swinging a blanket at an imaginary bull. With the temperature in the teens, we closed off all rooms that were not necessary to heat in the evenings.

* * *

The twenty-second of January, late in the afternoon, I started having labor pains. Jimmy called the hospital and spoke to an obstetrics nurse, she told him to bring me to the hospital. We had to find a babysitter for Melanie and Jason. Jimmy's Mom and dad were home and came over to stay with the children. They could be put to sleep in their own beds. It was a Sunday afternoon. Bursting with excitement, Jimmy assured them, "I'll call and let y'all know as soon as we see the doctor, your momma and the baby will be fine."

At that time, we had a copper tone dial phone on the wall in the kitchen and a princess phone on our bedside table, I can't even begin to describe the color of the phone in our bedroom, my best guess is yellowish gold. It is still on a shelf in our closet and I couldn't come up with a better description even holding it in my hands. It has a circular center with push buttons. In 1978, it would be long distance for Jimmy to call when he had news, and long distance was expensive, so the call would be brief.

Opening the car door, he helped me get settled and off to Augusta and University Hospital we went.

At that time there was a big problem with trains crossing Walton Way and that was the street we had to take to the hospital. If there was a train crossing the street, we could be stuck sitting there for fifteen or twenty minutes. My pains were getting harder. I just prayed no trains would interrupt our trip. Thankfully, the street was clear as we slowed over the bumpy double tracks.

Jimmy took me straight to the emergency entrance, I was checked for my progress and sent to the ob/gyn floor. That was about six o'clock in the evening, Jimmy sat beside my bed as darkness started to descend outside, the windows in the hospital room fogged because of the extreme temperature difference, heat versus extreme cold outdoors.

My labor pains just dragged on, I did receive some pain relief through the drip of the IV fluids, a port inserted in the back of my hand. Every time the nurse checked to see how far along I was, there was no progress. Finally, by midnight, my doctor, instructed the nurse to give me something to stop my contractions.

Dr. Bruns told my nurse, "Let Mrs. Widener get some rest, we'll induce labor in the morning." Heavenly relief, no pain and I began to drift off to sleep.

My eye lids felt like weights, forcing them to close. "Go home, Jimmy, and get some rest, check on our children. Be over here at nine in the morning."

At first, he protested and didn't won't to leave me. By the time he decided, I was sound asleep. I barely remember his words, "Good night, sweetheart, I'll see you in the morning." A brief kiss and he was gone.

* * *

The next morning, Monday, January 23, dawned clear and very cold.

A nurse entered and said, "Dr. Bruns wants me to break your water and we will give you medication through the IV to induce labor. Things should go pretty quickly."

She was certainly right about that. Jimmy walked in about 8:30 and I was having pounding labor pains. They began at the center of my back, traveled around my belly to meet in a crescendo of pain at my mid-section. The pain was so intense, I could only deal with it by twisting in the bed and shaking my feet, just any movement of my body to escape concentrating on the pain. I couldn't talk to my husband, only hold his hand, squeezing like a vice when the pain hit. I had nothing to relieve the pain at this point, Dr. Bruns did not want a repeat of the night before.

About 11:00, I told Jimmy to go downstairs and get some food, he had gotten out of bed, came straight to the hospital, no breakfast.

By 11:30, my nurse came to examine me, once again. I was in so much pain.

"We'll be taking you to delivery soon."

"Please find my husband, he went downstairs for something to eat, I can't go until he's here," writhing in pain, straining to get the words out.

"Don't worry, we'll have him in the Delivery Room when you get there."

I was soon pushed out the door, down the hall, heading for the delivery room. Entering, I barely noticed the bright lights over the operating table because of the excruciating pain. Dr. Bruns was there prepared to deliver my baby. Jimmy stood at the head of the table, with booties, mask, head covering, and gown over his street clothes. He was ready to see our child born. This was the first child birth he was allowed to witness. Dr. Bruns had a mirror so Jimmy was able to watch the delivery. Dr. Bruns gave me an epidural and my pain soon disappeared. Jimmy held my hands behind my head, a nurse took pictures of the whole procedure and our daughter, Lori Paige was born. It was 12:14 PM, just after noon.

That nurse taking photos with our camera had helped Jimmy get suited up for entering the delivery room. Asking him, "Mr. Widener are you sure you want to be in the delivery room, can you take it?" Fair question. I'm sure fathers had previously fainted or passed out. My husband answered her question, "I've helped my Daddy on the farm deliver heifers, I'll be fine."

To which the nurse replied, "Mr. Widener, your wife is no heifer."

28. Another Precious Life

Paige was born on Monday, January 23, she and I were scheduled to go home on Friday, the 27th. She lay on my hospital bed, dressed in her fancy, yellow dress with rows of white ribbon edged with lace and embroidered with tiny flowers and green stems. The rubber lined pants were decorated with the same. A matching bonnet tied under her chin with yellow ribbons covered her sparse, but very dark hair. Her Granny Peggy bought this outfit especially for the trip home. She lay there seemingly quiet content, covered by a croqueted green and white shawl her Aunt Lu had made. What a little angel she was laying there, tiny hands balled into fists on either side of her head.

I remember standing in front of the big window, waiting to be discharged, looking at a cloudless blue sky. With the fourth-floor view, it seemed I could see forever.

As soon as we got home, the fancy dress and pants were replaced with a thick terry zip up sleeper. Something more comfortable and we took pictures, Melanie and Jason took turns holding their little sister. I still have the pictures, of course, in a scrapbook.

***

At first Paige slept in a basinet in our room, then graduated to the same crib Melanie and Jason had occupied in her big sister's room. I believe she was talking before she could walk. Her Papa J.A. always called her, "My little talking baby." By age four, not only did she talk non-stop, but to the point, if I wanted a nap in the afternoon, I had to pay her fifty cents to be quiet for thirty minutes. She could also tell time. By first grade, she was reading and reciting parts of the movies, *Grease*, *Annie*, and even *Gone with the Wind*. In an exaggerated southern voice, she mimicked Aunt Pittypat's line, "Yankees in Georgia, how did they ever get in?"

I will always remember; we had a Christmas Cantata and play at Windsor church. The pews were packed that night. At the close, before Pastor Wingate dismissed with prayer, he announced, "We have a little lady who wants to recite the Christmas story to the congregation from the book of Luke. Paige, come forward." We did not know she had asked if she could do this until she got up marched down the aisle and stepped onto the pulpit. She stood there, like a practiced speaker and recited Luke 2:1-13. Afterward, to tremendous applause, she smiled, bowed her head and returned to her seat. It was unbelievable, we were so proud of that little five-year-old, she didn't stammer or miss a word.

Paige was always the consummate entertainer; she loved to laugh and make people laugh. She was a very precocious child, reading books even in the bathtub at night. Jimmy would knock on the door and say, "Paige, put that book down and get out of the tub."

We never know what tomorrow holds. Paige left a trail of broken hearts, like bread crumbs on the road of her life. She went sailing through life like there was no tomorrow, despair in her wake. I believe God is always in control; things always happen for a reason.

Paige is gone now, a loss my heart will never overcome, but I am a believer, therefore I accept whatever God intends in my life.

Jimmy and Kathy cutting their Wedding cake—June 28, 1969

Daddy, Momma, Bride Kathy, Groom Jimmy Widener and his parents Peggy and J.A. Widener

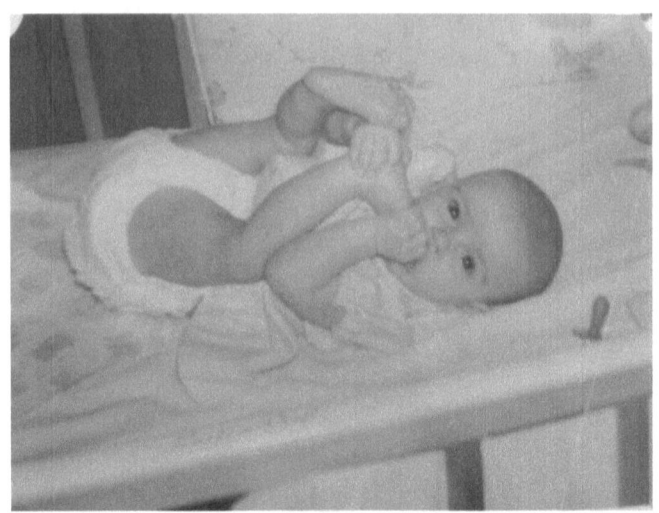

Melanie Lynn Widener in her crib 1970

*All Eight of Us. Willette, Kathy, Lula Mae, Linda and Louise. (Back row)
The boys, Big Steve, Little Steve and Donnie 1971 (Front row)*

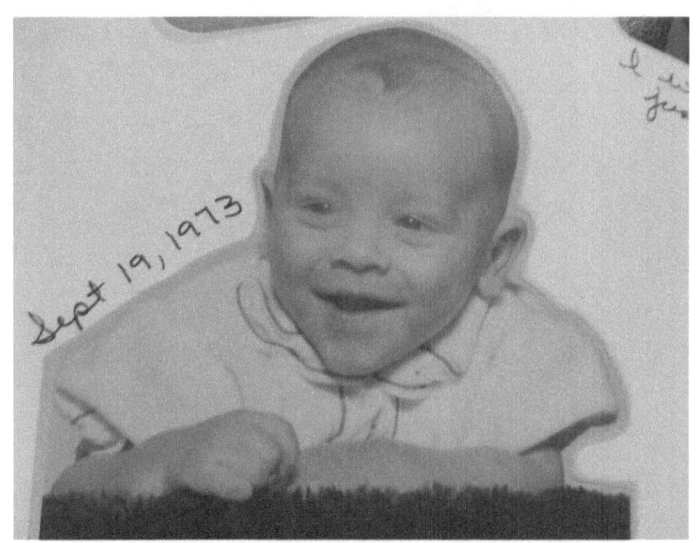

Jason Allen Widener

Jimmy holding Lori Paige Widener—January 23, 1978

Kathy Widener

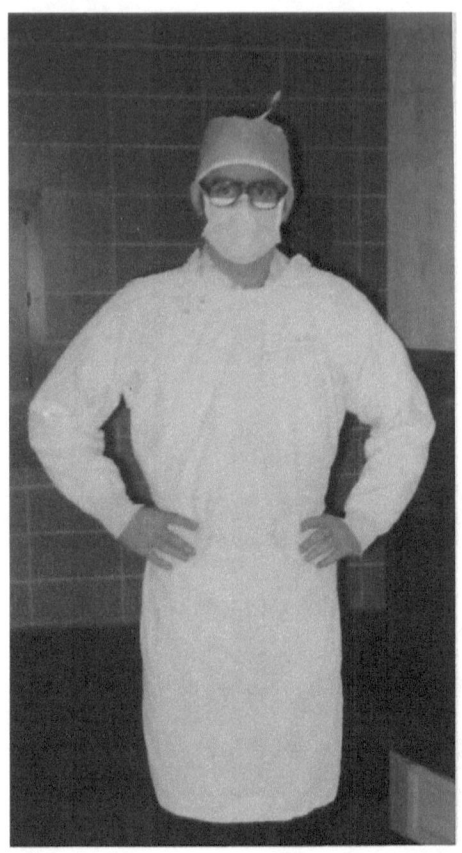

Jimmy ready to go in the Delivery Room — University Hospital, Augusta GA

29. Remembering Those Who Went Before

Because of my interest in genealogy and research, I began to apply and join organizations dependence on pedigree. I could, by this time, prove descent from many ancestors. The first group I joined was the UDC (United Daughters of the Confederacy) as a charter member of the newly created Jefferson Davis Chapter. This took place in 1982, we met at St. John's Methodist church, a small group of like-minded women who were proud of their ancestry. There were, of course, other chapters before this, in Aiken, but the members had all passed away and their Edward Croft Chapter was disbanded. Their membership had literally died of old age.

I joined under my great, great grandfather Thomas Jefferson Woodward, who was captured at the battle of the crater Petersburg, Virginia and sent to Elmira Prison in New York, he died there and is buried in Woodlawn Cemetery among rows of other Confederate headstones. He went away to war and never came back. My great grandmother, Peninnah, never knew what happened to her father. This was commonplace on both sides of the fight, blue and grey. I have dozens of Confederate soldiers in my family tree, but was not concerned with buying more pins for my red and white insignia ribbon. I joined mostly for the camaraderie. We were all very interested in genealogy. All the ancestors I have discovered were not rich, eking a living from the soil, farmers, not business men or plantation owners. None to my knowledge had slaves. They worked the land themselves.

The research was absolutely fascinating. Even without the internet, I was able to find documents, births recorded in family Bibles, death certificates, land deeds, and cemetery records. It was a constant passion. Our children kidded that their Dad went to junkyards searching for old cars and their Momma spent her free time in cemeteries.

Eventually, I also joined The Daughters of 1812, as a descendant of Russell Gunter. He was the original owner of the family land at Rayflin, lived to be ninety-eight years old, was a mason, and married Elizabeth Nelson from Orangbergh District. His wife lived to be ninety-five. They certainly did not eat healthy by today's standard. Their diet consisted of lots of fried foods, all deep fried in hog lard, vegetables from their own garden, even their pork sausage, after hanging in the smokehouse was cut into links packed in jars filled to the brim with grease and sealed. They had to have good genetics, plus the fact everything was organic, no pesticides on their vegetables, animals were all grass fed. Russell died in 1876, which means he was born two years after The Declaration of Independence was signed. He also received a pension for his service in the War of 1812.

In 1983, I applied for membership in the Trenton Chapter, Daughters of the American Revolution. The chapter was named after the Battle of Trenton, New Jersey when George Washington and his troops crossed the Delaware in freezing weather. Their boats were surrounded by floating ice and buffeted by battering winds. It was very dangerous, but morale was low for the American forces and Washington deemed it important for morale. The desperate attempt on the night of December 25th caught the Hessian troops garrisoned there unaware. The Continental's crossing was a success. The next morning, December 26, 1776, the battle was fought and won by Washington's forces. Though the numbers were not large, it ignited a flame and more rebels joined the cause for independence. It was a small but decisive victory for the Continental Army. The Trenton Chapter was founded in the early 1900's and is still going strong.

* * *

I actually found my niche when I researched my Gantt family and found my Quaker ancestry. My 5th great grandfather, Israel Gauntt, moved from New Jersey to North Carolina, then Camden, South Carolina, thence to Newberry. He was listed for patriotic service, providing supplies to Continental troops and local militia fighting the redcoats. Most of my involvement centered around the DAR. I met some very interesting people, some with fascinating stories to tell.

There were lots of luncheons, banquets, and monthly meetings. At these get-togethers, I talked to some ladies who were quite willing to share their claims to fame. All the ladies I met, some in my chapter, some in other chapters at district and state meetings, told amazing stories about brushes with famous people.

I sat beside a lady, don't remember her name, who told of her childhood in New Jersey and attending a state fair where a pilot offered to take anyone up for a fee. Her father paid for her to take a plane ride. Her pilot - Amelia Earhart.

A lady I dearly loved, from Kentucky, Mills Waterfill Merche dated the grandson of President William McKinley. Mills was a member of my DAR chapter.

There was another luncheon conversation with an Aiken lady

that was very noteworthy. She was a high school student in Aiken during the 1940's. One day she and a friend were walking down the sidewalk. The friend asked, "Do you know who lives in that house up ahead? Fred Astaire lives there; I dare you to go knock on his door."

The lady decided to take that dare, she ran up the steps, knocked on the door, ready to run away. The person that opened the door was the famous Mr. Astaire himself.

"Hello young lady," he said looking down at the trembling teenager.

"Sorry to bother you, sir, my friend dared me to knock on your door."

"No problem. Say would you mind waltzing a few steps with me right here on my porch."

"Gee, no sir, that would be swell, something to tell all my friends about."

Mr. Astaire waltzed a few times in circles with the brave teenager in his arms. "Now, you can tell all of your friends, you have waltzed with Fred Astaire."

A big smile brightened his face and the face of the teenage girl.

Also, a member of my chapter and a dear friend was Miss Ola Hitt. Ola spent her whole life in Aiken. A very patriotic lady, she worked a lot with veterans and ran a veteran's home on Chesterfield Street. Miss Ola was considered by many as the first lady of Aiken. For years she rode in a convertible and led the Memorial Day Parade. There is a room at the Aiken Historical Museum dedicated to the home where Ola and her siblings grew up. Pascalina. It is located outside of Montmorenci, with a historical marker beside Highway 78. The house served as headquarters for the Yankee General, Kilpatrick, during the battle of Aiken. It is now owned by the Heath family and the location of the Herb Fair in May and October.

Every Life Tells a Story

I was so glad I became a friend of Ola's. She drove a car until she reached one hundred years of age, even renewing her driver's license for ten more years before that monumental birthday. She always had a man's fedora hat under the rear window of her car, so everyone would have the impression that she had a male protector.

The first three years I attended DAR Continental Congress in Washington D.C., Ola donated money to my travel fund, and let me borrow her spinning wheel pin that anchored all DAR insignia ribbons. The pin she entrusted me with had belonged to Miss Elizabeth Teague, a favorite teacher at Aiken High. The street beside the football stadium is named for her. The pin Miss Teague had left to Ola was 14K gold, very old and very expensive.

Miss Ola passed away in 2012 at the age of 103, didn't make it to one hundred and ten, but a street on the southside of Aiken is named for her. Oh, I almost forgot, Ola had a claim to fame too. She worked at one of the stores downtown and sold Minnie Pearl her famous straw hat with the tag still on it. If you are too young to know who Minnie Pearl was, Google her.

30. Sights and Sounds of Washington D.C.

Every year the South Carolina state DAR organized a trip to Washington D.C. I was fortunate to ride the bus to Washington beginning in 1985. That first year we all stayed at the Holiday Inn in Georgetown. It was an adventure, filled with fun and experiences I had never dreamed of.

The bus left from Greenville early on a Saturday morning in April. Continental Congress, the official name, chose April and always the week that included April 19. That month was important because the first battle of the Revolutionary War was fought at Lexington and Concord on that day and month in 1775, 'The shot heard around the World' as described by Ralph Waldo Emerson in his Concord Hymn. Of course, a number of inconsistencies in the story as to involvement of militia and farmers, the number of deaths on both sides, even the famous ride of Paul Revere have come into question. His ride was described by Henry Wadsworth Longfellow in "Paul Revere's Ride" but may not have happened the way our history books record it. It most certainly does espouse the fact that an individual, like Paul Revere, can change the course of history. And that is the story of America. One person, always, can make an impact on the course of historic events if circumstances and Providence deem it so.

Our bus made stops from the upstate Greenville, Clinton to Columbia and northeast to Dillion, SC. From there we crossed into North Carolina, following I-95 through Virginia and into our Nation's Capital. Ladies from the Charleston area met the bus in Dillion. Our driver and the bus were retained for seven days. We left on Saturday, rode all day, stopping for lunch about midway across North Carolina. And of course, at least once for gas. Ladies brought snacks and we had a cooler full of cold drinks on the back seat of the bus. We pulled into our hotel around 7:00 P.M., tired from a ten-hour bus ride.

The first year I attended, 1985, was the most exciting week of my life, thus far. For me, at least, it was nothing short of awesome. There were five pages from SC who attended that first year. Each page was between the ages of eighteen and thirty-six. Pages always wore white dresses with a blue and white ribbon draped from right shoulder to waist and pinned there. The word Page was emblazoned in white letters across the DAR blue ribbon. Pages had a variety of jobs, all intended to make the convention run smoother. We were ushers, door openers, coat checkers, flower deliverers, support for the credential committee, assigned to hallways, the library, entrance and exit doors, and of course, message carriers for all DAR ladies. It was our job and we were expected to stay on our feet when working, especially the evening sessions.

Opening night was Monday, April 15 at 8:30. Every page was dressed in formal white attire with elbow length gloves. Every attendee dressed formally also. Men wore tuxedoes or at least suit and tie. Ladies could wear long or short dresses, but all were fancy. There was a special night for National Defense and State Regents night when each state was represented on stage by their Regent. They stood center stage in Constitution Hall to report on their state's progress for the year. There were many luncheons, banquets, and teas that took place during the week, every state put on some event, most took place at the Capitol Hilton, the official DAR headquarters for dignitaries and important presenters.

On Opening Night, I was so excited stepping off the bus in the parking area at Constitution Hall. The night air was chilly and perfumes competed in the night breeze. Sweet smells surrounded us as we headed for the main entrance. I had never seen so many sequined, lace, silk, brocade, and satin gowns in one place, ever. The ladies were frosted with diamond necklaces, broaches, earrings, or strings of pearls. Matching sequined high heels, evening shoes of silver and gold adorned their feet. Most carried small evening bags; many ladies wore mink wraps or jackets draped from their shoulders. No plain clothing was worn, not for opening night. It was like stepping through a mirror into a fairy tale with all the fancy jewelry, fine clothes, and high-class ladies and gentlemen surrounding me.

Something else assaulted my senses that night. As we paraded down the sidewalk, admiring all the glitter and glitz, chatting and complementing our fellow attendees, I detected a whiff of something unexpected. A strong smell of unwashed body and filthy clothing hit my nose. We passed a heat vent beside that sidewalk, a man sat there for the warmth, head down, ignoring the chatter and laughter. He was a homeless person, the first one I had ever seen in a big city. I knew about hobos who rode the rails and camps during the depression where dirty, down and out folks lived in shacks, but to me this was different.

I had never seen homeless people on the streets before, as I would that week in Washington D.C. That Opening Night was something amazing and was only marred by my face-to-face revelation of what homelessness looks like.

Kathy Widener

* * *

As we entered the grand lobby of Constitution Hall, gold stars on the floor and blue and gold striped wallpaper, ladies milled around laughing and talking. The U.S. Marine Band was set up in front below the stage. They were playing lively patriotic music, all states had assigned seating which was alternated each year, floor to tiers that reached to the ceiling, the nose bleed section as we called it. Every delegate and attendee was handed a program as we entered. Inside was a map of the floor which showed where each state was to be seated. The program also lists the events for the week and what business would be taken up in the morning, afternoon, and evening sessions. As a new page, I was directed to steps going down to the basement level. A door marked, Pages Only, was a large room where new pages signed in, my name had been sent to the Page Committee from my state. There were bathrooms, dressing areas, and a desk for the Director of Pages. I was given my ribbon to wear and assigned as an usher at one of the side doors that led into the main hall.

Reporting to my assigned section, I entered, walked up steps, entering the main arena just like entering a football stadium. The capacity of Constitution Hall was three thousand seven hundred people and there were few empty seats. Two other pages assigned to this entrance greeted me as I walked in; our job was to help ladies find their seats. The band played on while attendees were being seated. There were already dignitaries seated on the stage. They had entered from The President General's Reception Room to the left of the stage. We were waiting for the grand processional, twenty-one Vice President Generals and the grand dame herself, President General Sarah King from Tennessee. Sprinkled throughout this processional were pages escorting each group.

Every Life Tells a Story

The United States Marine Band began the grand march music, John Phillip Sousa's Stars and Stripes forever. As the President General got close to the front, the band reached the crescendo, movement in the ceiling caught my eye. Just as Mrs. King reached a particular spot, an arm from the ceiling dropped an American flag, Old Glory unfurled at precisely the right moment and waved above the head of Mrs. King. It was a huge flag and slowly raised toward the ceiling on a tether. It was nothing short of magnificent, the highlight of the evening in my eyes. I was thinking, every patriotic American should witness this: The Stars and Stripes march, the huge flag floating down from the ceiling and the audience on their feet, cheering and clapping. It was a glorious entrance and beginning to Continental Congress. How could it possibly get better? But it did.

* * *

By the time we got back to the Holiday Inn, we were all too excited to sleep. There were just too many things to talk about, we gathered in small groups in our rooms, finery tossed aside, most of us had on our pajamas and robes. We needed to get comfortable and chat about our impressions. It was really a gossip fest about what others said and did, never mean, but always honest about our opinions. We sipped wine or mixed drinks and munched on peanuts and snacks.

The DAR was known for having dynamic speakers, mostly powerful politicians. Senator Al Gore Jr. from Tennessee was the speaker that night. Senator Gore was from Mrs. King's home state of Tennessee, he and his wife, Tipper Gore sat on the stage.

For two nights in a row that week, I went to sleep at three A.M. and had to be ready and on the bus at 8:00 the next morning. I was not the only one, but you can do that when you are young, and I was. We had to be at the Hall at 9:00 for the business meeting, in our white attire and at our duty stations.

* * *

A White House tour was planned for Tuesday at 2:00 P.M. Ronald Reagan was President and this was a special tour indeed. Only members of the DAR were allowed in that day.

If you have ever been fortunate to take a White House tour, tickets are required, at no cost, in advance, and have to be requested from your Congressman or some high up political person. I went on a White House tour once with a genealogical group. My ticket was issued by Lee Atwater's office, a campaign consultant for Ronald Reagan, George Bush Sr. and once Chairman of the Republican party. Lee was a hometown guy having grown up in Aiken, South Carolina. I never met him. He tragically died of cancer in 1991 at age 40.

On a regular White House tour, a guide accompanies a small group of people, and introduces them to each room on the main floor. The rooms are roped off, visitors only get to look inside as the guide explains the significance of each room and the furnishings, no photos allowed. That was the way it was done in the 1990's.

When the DAR toured the White House in 1985, it was very different. We entered through the east wing visitor's foyer, visited the China Room where a place setting of every Presidents china is on display, the Blue Room, Red Room, Green Room, East Room, and the State Dining Room. There were no ropes up, we could roam freely, sit on the furniture and take photographs. There was a Secret Service agent in each room to answer our questions, even had a picture taken with one of the agents in the Red Room. I also have a picture sitting in the President's chair in the State Dining Room. I asked the agent in the room, "Which chair is President Reagan's?"

He replied, "Try the one with the arm rests."

It was a fantastic experience. I'm thinking the DAR was pretty important at that time and we all felt special visiting the people's house.

* * *

I was a page in Washington at Continental Congress for three years before I aged out, too old to serve. Every one of those years, we were invited to a Page's event in appreciation for our service. That first year, 1985, was the best. We were invited to visit the Capitol and a reception following. White evening gowns were not a requirement that night. I wore a long sleeveless satin V-neck aqua gown with a wrap-a-round skirt and satin sash to match that I had made myself. We had a couple of Secret Service agents that directed us. First, we were allowed to sit on the floor of the House of Representatives, "an honor" our guide told us. He said only one-half percent of all Americans get to do that. No pictures allowed, but since the five of us were leaving last we stepped up beside the podium and had someone take one anyway. I have that picture in a scrapbook. There were no cell phones at that time, so no selfies.

I attended every Continental Congress from 1985 until 1997. I have great pictures, great memories. We rode the metro, visited the Smithsonian Museums, attended luncheons, teas, and banquets, Arlington National Cemetery, Arlington House, and the Tomb of the Unknown Soldier. Two friends and I took a train from Union Station in Washington to Baltimore. We visited Mt. Vernon and Thomas Jefferson's home, Monticello, the National Archives where we saw the original Declaration of Independence and the Constitution. We rode a city bus just for fun and many taxis, first time I rode in a taxi. We walked the streets of Washington, visited the National Zoo and the Vietnam Memorial where we located the name of Harold Renwick on that black marble wall of valor. He was the husband of one of our DAR ladies. These are experiences I will always treasure.

As far as the sights and sounds of Washington: I can remember pink cherry blossoms showering into the tidal basin, the smell of exhaust from city buses, the black smoke that swirled from their tail pipes as they headed to the next stop. The applause, almost deafening when the flag dropped from the ceiling, the speeches I attended for speakers: Bill Bennett, Congressman Charles Rob and Lynda Baines Johnson, his wife, daughter of LBJ, David Eisenhower and wife Julia Nixon Eisenhower, Sandra Day O'Connor, Jeanne Kirkpatrick, Warren Burger, Oliver North, Jack Kemp, Shirley Temple Black, and Gene Cernan, the last astronaut to walk on the moon. I also, with some friends, visited Congressman Arthur Ravenel from Charleston, Senator Strom Thurmond, and of course my kinsman, Congressman Floyd Spence. If you don't recognize these names, you clearly need to study more U.S. history. In 1987, Easter Sunday, I took a picture of a cross arranged with potted Easter Lilies on the steps of the U.S. Capitol. That would not happen in today's political climate.

I am an optimist. Benjamin Franklin asked this question at the signing of the Declaration of Independence in Independence Hall, Philadelphia, referring to the chairs at the signing table, a Sun carved into the top of the backboard of the chair, "I wonder is that a rising sun or a setting sun?" I don't know what the decision was, but I believe it is obvious now that it was a rising sun and I choose to believe Americans still envision a rising sun.

31. The First Time I Ever Flew

"It's only when you're flying above it that you
realize how incredible the Earth really is"
— *Phillip Perrin*

We headed to the airport in Columbia, South Carolina. We had to be there very early, before the blush of dawn even began to tint the eastern sky. It was still velvety black except for the stars shining above and the scattered street lights. After we parked, Louise, daughter Charity, my daughter Melanie and I exiting the car, headed for the terminal. It was hot. Even with the darkness, it held promise for a steamy day in South Carolina. Mid-September 1984, the coolness of fall was still a month away. Even, at that early hour, the temperature was stifling. We had no luggage, only our handbags, camera cases, and tote bags containing jackets, a book and enough space for small souvenirs. Charity and Melanie carried nothing. We were absolutely ecstatic, we were flying to Buffalo, New York on a guided tour to visit Niagara Falls. It was a one-day guided tour we had planned and paid for months before. We would have a tour guide and our own bus waiting at the airport in Buffalo.

The four of us were all flying for the first time, I definitely had butterflies in my stomach. This flying thing was exciting, but frightening at the same time. The airline was Eastern, all the way; Columbia to Atlanta, then to Buffalo, New York where we would meet our bus. It had to be planned down to the smallest detail, that was our tour guide's department. It was a one-day trip and we would be back in Columbia late that night.

As soon as we were seated in the commercial airliner, which we had entered from the tarmac up a set of steps, we settled in our seats, ready for a new experience. After the plane ascended, so far above the earth, the sun soon began to light up the eastern sky and the ground far below. In thirty minutes or so we were descending to land at Atlanta's Hartfield International Airport. I had read that at certain times of the day, it is the busiest airport in the world. We stayed together as a group and had no problems locating our next gate, since all Eastern Airline planes were assigned to the same concourse. This time we entered from an extended sleeve to step into our plane.

I was sitting next to the window when we left Atlanta. By then it was good daylight, and I immediately realized this was something I would always love. The earth below really did look like a checker board with fields, forests, and bodies of water spread before me like a carpet, all different shapes and sizes. I could see highways as the daylight took over, little tiny vehicles traveling far below looked like crawling ants.

The airtime to Buffalo was only two hours. I thought to myself, how amazing is it to fly that far that fast? About an hour into the flight we were above the clouds, the earth disappeared. I could see wispy white puffs, like cotton, drift past my window. I remembered all the trips we had taken as children up winding mountain roads in North Carolina, elevations above the clouds, no comparison, however, to 25,000 feet up.

The pilot soon announced we would be beginning our descent

to the airport in Buffalo, New York. As we passed through the cloud cover, Lake Erie was spread before us. To me, I thought maybe we were over the ocean. Lake Erie is not nearly the largest of the Great Lakes, but all I could see from my small plane window was a huge body of brown water. We soon were over land again, the city of Buffalo. Seat belt lights flashing, slowing of air speed and the sound of the landing gear lowering filled my senses. Slowly the plane descended, touching down to a gray, cloudy day in Buffalo. We descended from the plane via a set of steps pushed to the main cabin door, between the cockpit and first class. The pilot and co-pilot were there to wish us a great day and of course our airline stewardesses, all young, slim, and attractive. At that time, 1984, there were strict standards as to height, age, and weight of flight attendants. As we stepped onto the tarmac, we spotted our green tour bus and headed, as a group, in that direction. It was thirty-eight degress with a misting rain falling, big difference from South Carolina.

We landed in Buffalo about 10:30 A.M. With traffic, it was about a thirty-minute drive to our main destination. First stop was the American side and Niagara Falls. The group boarded the Maid of the Mist for a boat trip to the very base of the plunging river of water. As we stepped onto the boat, each passenger was handed a thick black rain coat with hood and black rain boots. Of course, these were one size fits all, so they were hugh on each of us. The ride to the Falls was scary, loud, and we immediately saw the need for the rain gear, we all got soaked. It was a really fun experience and we laughed a lot.

After the Maid of the Mist, our bus driver drove us along the Niagara River, pointing out Goat Island which lies on the American side between Niagara Falls and Bridal Veil Falls. Goat Island is part of Niagara Falls State Park and is open to the public, we did not however, due to time constraints, actually go to the island. That would have to be another trip. We did stop along the river and took pictures.

Next planned attraction was crossing the border into Canada where we would be served lunch. We crossed the Rainbow Bridge, stopped at the Canadian border where an agent entered our bus, asked a few questions of our tour guide and looked at all adults' United States drivers licenses. At that time, no passport was required and I don't believe the girls had to have an ID.

The agent was only on the bus five minutes and cleared us to cross into Canada.

There was a tall building in Niagara Falls, Canada, about four stories. We took an elevator to the top where a buffet lunch had been prepared for us. Of course, the view from the top floor windows was magnificent. When finished with lunch, we took the elevator to street level and stepped outside, crossing the street to an overlook with an astonishing view of Horseshoe Falls on the Canadian side. Lots of oohs and ahs from the whole group. On thing most apparent to me was the loud sound of the plunging water as the Niagara River dropped over the abrupt escarpment. We were given a brief opprtunity to linger and absorb through all our senses what beauty lay before us. The sight of the curtain of water pouring unceaseingly, the sound so loud it was almost impossible to hear the comments of those around us, the touch of the slipperty, wet iron rail between us and the cliff's edge and the taste as water splashed against the huge rocks below and sprayed our faces.

Reluctantly we boarded our tour bus. Next stop, a souvenir shop to purchase some little mementos from our trip. Loading our group aboard the tour bus once again we back tracked across the border at the Rainbow Bridge, this time stopping briefly for American border agents.

Every Life Tells a Story

Our trip to Niagara Falls is a wonderful memory. As we again left the bus, walked acrosss the tarmac, and climbed steps to our Eastern airliner for the trip home, the pilot of our plane asked Melanie and Charity if they would like to sit in the pilot's seat and have their picture taken. Melanie's picture is in her scrapbook today.

The trip home, every one of our group was on an emotional high. We experienced a wonderful day full of sunshine and beauty. We saw Niagara Falls and Horseshoe Falls, had lunch, a driving tour, and sailed aboard the Maid of the Mist. The cost of this one-day excursion including the airfare, per person, was $100.00. Well worth that, I would say. We arrived safely late at night in Columbia after a brief lay-over in Atlanta. I read somewhere, "If you're going to Hell, you have to go through Atlanta." Of course, that's a bit ridiculous, and said in jest, but Atlanta is really a big hub for air travel.

We never had our purse scanned, had to remove our shoes or walk through metal detectors. Times have really changed since that first plane trip. Mostly, I believe, because of 9-11 when terrorists hijacked planes and destroyed the Twin Towers in New York. We learned a hard lesson that day, we can no longer be complacent, we have to do things differently to ensure our safety. I'll always remember that first plane trip, what fun and how innocent Americans were back then.

32. Back to School

"An investment in knowledge pays the best interest"
Benjamin Franklin

In the spring of 1987, eighteen years after I graduated from high school, I went to college. Personal home computers were just becoming popular.

Jimmy told me, "If you go to USC Aiken and take a computer course, I'll buy us a computer." I readily agreed. Melanie was finishing her junior year at South Aiken high school; Jason was in 9th grade and Paige was in middle school. I had been a stay-at-home mom for years, picking up kids from school, taking them to doctor and dental appointments, jazz, tap, ballet, and gymnastics classes, cooking and cleaning. I was ready to try something new. I still enjoyed genealogy, and the historical organizations I held memberships in. Melanie had a car and drove to school in the mornings taking Jason and Paige, so I no longer had that chore.

I took placement tests in English and Math and did well enough that I did not have to take remedial classes. That was a surprise considering I had not taken a class since high school. I figured out really quick; the shorthand class I took was a waste of my time. Typing however came in good with computers, the keyboard was basically the same as a typewriter.

My computer class met Monday, Wednesday, and Fridays. My professor, Dr. Kapranedis was a nice guy, a patient instructor. He was at least ten years my senior, gray bushy hair, beard, and a foreigner from Greece with a distinct accent. Of course, I did not fault him for that, I have a pretty distinct accent myself, and he spoke at least two languages, I just speak one, Southern English.

The Computer Concepts class was supposed to teach us how to write a program that would bounce a yellow ball on a screen. The operating system was DOS which used floppy disc, there were no colored monitors, just a huge cumbersome box resembling a TV, keyboard, and desktop PC tower where information was stored. I don't remember a lot of particulars about the computers then. I know these were not the first computers by far, NASA and the government used computers, but they filled an entire room. In 1987, smaller three component personal computers were available for home use. The internet was not yet invented, but now we had our own personal computer.

What did we intend to use that first computer for? You could buy programs and install yourself. I purchased a program from the Church of Jesus Christ of the Latter-day Saints. It would allow the user to keep track of genealogy, input individual people, add birth and death records, add notes, source material, and connect families together. The program was called Personal Ancestral File. There were five or six discs with instructions for installation. To my surprise, I was able to follow the instructions and install the program myself. I immediately started entering names of relatives and connecting them in my database. When technology advanced further, I no longer used the program, but I had entered somewhere around 5,000 individuals. Typing white letters and numbers on a black screen became an obsession. I still have the actual computer tower in my closet, just in case.

Every Life Tells a Story

That first computer was only used for the PAF program and of course, playing, where in the World is Carmine San Diego?

***

After that first semester in 1987, I decided to continue with my studies. I loved literature and history, so I decided to attend part-time. My major would be History. Sometimes I would take two classes a semester, sometimes more, but I studied.

College classes were rewarding. I knew nothing about art until Dr. Tom Mack's art history class. I can still recognize Monet's impressionist landscapes, Degas's famous ballerinas, Mary Cassatt's children, Warhol's Campbell soup cans, and Picasso's strange cubist paintings. Art, like beauty, is in the eye of the beholder. Who would have thought Jackson Pollock's splatted paint on canvas would be considered art?

I took literature classes in early English literature, Romanticism, and Realism. Tom Mack also taught my literature classes, which were most beneficial. We discussed John Woolman from Mt. Holly, N.J. This was pre-American Revolution. Mr. Woolman was a Quaker who wrote extensively about abolition of slavery. I trace my ancestry to the Quakers of Burlington County NJ. John Woolman grew up as a Quaker in the same region.

I enjoyed all three literature classes, reading Henry David Thoreau's, *Walden*, a man who enjoyed the solitude of the forest on Walden's pond. He wrote about his simple life and the quiet solace of existing in a natural setting. I still remember a quote of his, "The mass of men lead lives of quiet desperation." He was speaking of the need to have material things and wealth which does not make any man happy. I totally agreed with Mr. Thoreau on his quote.

I also recall trying to plow through Ralph Waldo Emerson's

essay, *Self-Reliance*. To me, it was the most boring piece of Mr. Emerson's work I ever read.

We read works of Herman Melville, Nathaniel Harthorne, and analyzed the poetry of Emily Dickinson. There were also the horrifying stories of author Edgar Allan Poe who wrote tales of mystery and death. The macabre was his specialty, *The Masque of the Red Death*, comes to mind and Poe's fascination with the subject of dying. Edgar Allan Poe's poem, *The Raven* envisions dread. Poe was reportedly so afraid of dying and being buried alive he requested a long rope, attached to a bell and inserted in his coffin at death. That is where we get the phrase, 'saved by the bell'. I equate his writing with our modern-day Stephen King.

My other classes were mostly history, Western Civilization, History of the United States which included the Korean Conflict, and our involvement in Vietnam, Southern Studies, and The Constitution. I was always eager to learn new facts, that's why I read all my required reading assignments and did the required writing tasks. The most memorable class to me was Southern Studies taught by Dr. Brockington, also my advisor. He climbed onto the desk and demonstrated the Shag, South Carolina's official dance. The class was held in a theater style classroom so all students could watch those Shag steps. We also had group discussions about the differences in BBQ, the kind of sauce popular in different regions of the South, and music, country versus Southern Rock. When discussing country music, every song tells a story.

I really loved going to classes and was proud when I received an Associate's Degree with High Honors in August 1990. I completed sixty-seven hours and was a member of the Honor Society at USC Aiken. I did not continue for a Bachelor's degree in History. It was more for my own gratification and my children were going to college, I felt like I was too old to start a new career and also pay for their college education. But I have never regretted the time I spent in study and reading. It made me a better person, both in the knowledge I gained and emotionally through interacting with students and faculty. I guess I needed to prove something to myself and I did.

33. Crossing the Pond

"Live your life by a compass not a clock."
—*Stephen Covey*

"To travel is to live."
—*Hans Christian Anderson*

My husband and I had never traveled very far. He had flown when we first married to New Orleans and San Antonio to fulfill his military obligation, I had flown to Buffalo, NY, but most of our trips were to the SC coast or to the mountains of North Carolina and Tennessee by car. My trips to Washington, D.C. had been exciting on the DAR bus, but that was about to change. I had heard DAR ladies talk about 'crossing the pond' and I eventually realized they were comparing the Atlantic Ocean to a pond.

I had never considered that we might actually need to apply for a passport one day, but in April 1996, we had a chance to cross that pond ourselves. Jason studied abroad during college in Bregenz, Austria, the fall of 1994, staying in an upstairs apartment with two other American guys. The three shared rent in a house where an older couple lived. The lady brought them scones and jam every morning, otherwise they had to buy their own food. We sent him several care packages with lots of instant cheese grits and plastic jars of peanut butter.

In the spring of 1996, he returned, staying with his friend, Wolfgang Winkler. They had met on his first trip and hit it off from the start, meeting in a pub in Bregenz over German beer. When Jason went back in 1996, Jimmy and I were invited by Wolfgang to visit and stay with him and Jason in his apartment in Wolfurt, Austria. Wolfurt is a small municipality clustered with other small towns around Lake Constance. The small villages actually run together, similar to boroughs around New York City. Austria, Germany, and Switzerland all border on the lake known as the Bodensee in German. We had met Wolfgang when he came to the U.S. in 1995 and were more than anxious to visit him in Austria. We would have two guides and interpreters, Jason and Wolfgang; also, Wolfgang offered us a place to stay.

On Sunday, April 14, 1996, Jimmy and I flew from Columbia, SC to Atlanta to begin a trip of a lifetime. Once we landed in Atlanta, we took a shuttle to the Best Western to spend the night, have a quiet dinner and prepare for the long overseas flight.

On Monday morning the hotel shuttle took us back to Atlanta Hartfield Airport to begin our trip. We flew United airlines from Atlanta to Dulles in Washington DC then on to Zurich, Switzerland to see Jason. He and Wolfgang would meet us at the airport in Zurich.

Dulles is one of two airports in Washington DC, the other being National, now Reagan National. We had some time to explore the airport, never getting too far from our gate. Both Jimmy and I were smokers at that time and were told there was a smokers' lounge where visitors could enjoy a cigarette. The lounge turned out to be a glass room in the middle of one of the throughfares, completely filled with smoke and benches around the inside glass wall. Peering through the glass walls, vision was blurred as a thick fog of gray hid smokers inside from pedestrians passing. Truthfully, you didn't even need to light a cigarette, just enter, find a seat and inhale. No smoke escaped when the door was opened, negative air flow, I believe. It was certainly not ideal for enjoying the smoking experience.

When we boarded our plane to leave Dulles, it was almost 6:30 in the evening and raining. Outside my small plane window, I could see splatters of rain, darkness, and a few lights shining from security poles, airport windows, and other planes landing and coasting off the runway. We took off into a stormy night with only the lights inside the plane, soon dimmed except for passengers reading, most seasoned travelers were trying to catch some nap time. The stewardesses had brought all passengers a small pillow and a blanket. They, of course, explained as soon as takeoff, the procedure in an emergency, where the exits were, demonstrated how the drop-down ceiling oxygen masks worked, and how to put them on. Of course, we had to take their word for the oxygen mask, we didn't see them, which of course was a good thing.

Nothing was visible on the ground after we reached cruising altitude. About 1:00 AM in the morning by my watch, we were beginning to see daylight heading to meet us from the east. Outside my plane window, I could barely make out the wing of our plane. Daylight was coming fast. Soon, I could see the patchwork of the earth below. Our pilot announced we were over eastern France. In the distance were the snow-covered mountains of the Alps, row upon row of snowy peaks jutting skyward, each higher than the previous.

We began our descent, almost 2:00 AM U.S. eastern time, 8:00 AM Zurich time. The plane seemed to float, like a feather in a light breeze, towards the runway, engine beginning to slow as we approached. We landed in Zurich April 16, 1996 to a beautiful sunny day.

As we disembarked from the wide-bodied jet, the pilot, co-pilot, and our stewardess were there to wish us a safe journey. This plane was for international travel, four seats in the center and two on either side. Entering the airport through the extended sleeve we entered a wide corridor; the walls and floor were black. Sunlight spilled through the large windows to our right, bright squares of light against the dark of the hall surface. These windows overlooked several United planes, including the one we had flown on. Dust motes danced in the bright shafts of sunlight and the skies above were azure and totally empty of drifting clouds. It was just an amazing clear day, sky so blue there seemed no limit above, only the sun, a bright disk too luminous to gaze upon.

Down the center of the corridor there were round display cases, topped with glass compartments filled with sparkling jewelry, Swarovski crystal, lights in the top of the displays illuminated the colors, absolutely beautiful. Just off the plane and already vying for travelers' cash. It did seem logical that international travelers had money. We, of course, were more interested in locating Jason and Wolfgang, we had no cell phone to call. As we walked to the end of the corridor we arrived at a huge room with a wide walkway. Set up like a mall, there was a chasm exposing a floor below. On the opposing side, across the way stood our son, Jason, and friend, Wolfgang, waving to get our attention. There were escalators to descend to the lower level where our baggage was to be claimed. Descending the escalators from our side and the guys from theirs' we met at baggage claims greeting them both with broad smiles and hugs all around. We collected our bags from the ever-revolving track, pushing the cart ladened with our belongings through customs, and presented our passports. We cleared easily, after answering a few questions, length of stay, our destination, and where we were staying. The only thing required before leaving was picking up the rental car from Alamo and signing the contract. We rented a small, red Opal station wagon, Jason would be our driver.

As we left the city heading for the Austrian border, my eyes were glued to the streets and people of Zurich. This was indeed an international city, known for Swiss chocolate, Swiss watches, and, of course, for Swiss Bank accounts. The streets were full of interesting people, cafes overflowed outdoors with tables and chairs on the sidewalk, flower sellers, newsstands, and specialty food vendors. The adventure was beginning.

34. Austria in Spring

> "Some old-fashioned things like fresh
> air and sunshine are hard to beat"
> —*Laura Ingalls Wilder*

> "All the Flowers of all the tomorrows
> are in the seeds of today"
> —*Unknown*

We arrived at Wolfgang's apartment building, two stories with twelve apartments, white with brown shutters, two main doors. Entering the entrance door to the right was Wolfgang's apartment on the first floor. There was a living room, his bedroom off the living area, a hallway, small kitchen to the right, then a bathroom, small but immaculate. Across from the bath, a second bedroom occupied by Jason. Jimmy and I were grateful that Wolfgang gave us his bedroom, sleeping in the living room himself on a blow-up mattress.

The view from the living area window was breath taking; imagine gazing on the snowy Alps from your window every day. The weather was wonderfully cool, except in the direct sunlight. We would consider it sweater weather in South Carolina. Every day during our ten days in Austria, I wore, at least, a button up sweater.

Just looking at the Alps gave me a chill. The bed where we slept had two pillows and one comforter. The first night, I wore sweat pants, sweat shirt and socks, after two nights, I slept in a tee shirt and my undies. I had no idea how warm one can be under a goose down comforter.

* * *

The tiny country of Liechtenstein was our destination our first full day in Austria. I had never heard of this small country until we actually visited. It lies between Switzerland and Austria and is slightly over 17 miles long and 7 miles wide. The capital city is Valduz, population five thousand. The government is a constitutional monarchy ruled by the monarch, Prince Hans-Adam II and a democratically elected parliament. The Prince lives in the castle on a hilltop overlooking the city. It is the royal family's private residence and is not open to the public. Visitors are allowed to drive up to the castle and take photos outside. The day we visited the castle, there were two men near the castle checking out a very expensive looking red sports car. Some of the royal family? Maybe, if so, they paid no attention whatsoever to three tourists posing for photos a hundred yards away.

We visited other ancient structures in the days to follow: Meersburg Castle, the oldest surviving in Germany, parts of which date to AD 630, a house in Meersburg still standing was built in 1692, the outside crisscrossed with brown lattice work, window shutters of red. We visited an ancient gothic church in Innsbruck, Austria. Marble columns of white with swirls of pink visible from bottom to top. These marble columns held up the walls inside the center portion, the roof had flying buttresses and orate carved tables and pews. There is a long line of life-size bronze cast statues, relatives of Emperor Ferdinand I, who had the church built for his final resting place in 1553.

The most impressive structure we visited was Neuschanstein Castle in the southern province of Germany, Bavaria. The castle was built by King Ludwig II in the late nineteenth century. The castle was made famous by the movie, The Monument Men. Hitler's army used Neuschansten to hide stolen works of art during WWII. The Cinderella castle at Disney World was also modeled after Ludwig's castle. It is a magnificent building. Sadly, King Ludwig only lived in this impressive palace about a month and a half before he died. But it still stands as a monument to the artisans that built it and now all visitors can enjoy the opulent furnishings, carvings, and paintings inside.

We were privileged to visit many towns around Lake Constance, Lindau, Germany, Feldkrich and Dornbirn, Austria and the larger city of Innsbruck. We had to drive through a pass in the snow-covered Alps to Innsbruck. We observed skiers on the packed snow below our elevated roadway and snow fences on the mountain sides to prevent the danger of avalanches.

Every town we visited, flower vendors bordered the streets offering a profusion of colors, varieties, and beauty, the sidewalks filled with tables and chairs for outside dining. There was no trash on the sidewalks or town centers, everything was unblemished by garbage or trash thrown from car windows or buses. The buildings were old and built for asthetic beauty. There were decorative shutters in multi colors, complicated rooflines, columns of marble or pillars of ancient brick. The people were very accommodating and friendly to tourists. The days were sunny, the mountains covered in spruce, meadows of grassland interspersed with the forest, snow covered at the higher elevations. Beauty was everywhere we looked. The air was crisp in the mornings and after the sun dipped low in the west. Many of the town streets were paved in gray bricks laid in circular patterns.

On our last day, as we left the apartment to meet Wolfgang at his favorite bar across the German border eight miles away; we were intercepted by three young children. Jason recognized them as kids who lived in the same apartment building. Being enterprising they had probably been observing the Americans for days and thought here was an opportunity to cash in on our generous nature. They sold us two rocks, small price to pay for their tenacity and smiles. Jason knelt beside them for a picture, still have the two rocks and the picture of the brave children.

Waldscheke' literally means forest bar. Shortly after crossing the German border from Bregenz, there was a small two rut road to the right which led into thick woods. A short way down this road, a building appeared with steps up the side and a large green sign, Waldscheke'. The second-floor bar had two rooms; one contained a well-stocked bar of liquors, wines, and a multitude of German beer selections. Stools lined one side of the beautifully carved bar where a few guys sat enjoying beer. The second room contained small tables with crisp white linen cloths and napkins. A full meal was not available but a tapas menu, small hors d'oeuvre and sandwiches were the main fare along with drinks. Patrons, of course, came for the atmosphere and the drinks.

At the bar on this particular night were two guys, one had a very prominent tattoo on his right arm revealed by sleeves torn from his jean jacket, ruddy complexion, clean shaven with a mane of reddish curls. He and his friend sat on stools at the bar. The friend had a small moustache and a mullet type haircut. They seemed to be amiable fellows, smiling and chatting while downing their beers.

Jimmy wanted to have a picture taken with the tattooed guy and went over and made the request. They of course seemed happy to oblige. Jimmy stood between them and one of our group took the picture. Just another example of the friendly and sociable charm of the Austrian/German people.

Still have that photo too.

We stayed rather late at the bar that night, drinking, talking, and laughing, much later than we should have. We had a great time, but realized it was our last night and knew our trip home had to begin early the next morning. We were scheduled to be at the airport in Zurich at 8:00A.M., thank goodness we had our bags already packed.

***

Thursday April 25, 1996

Jason was driving us to the airport in Zurich, Switzerland to catch our flight home. We hurriedly loaded the back of the small car, saying our final goodbyes to Wolfgang. The streets of Zurich were filled with people going about their daily lives. I watched through the car window, making memories of the sights and sounds of this beautiful city, spread in the shadow of the majestic Alps. I never expect to return. It was a beautiful city with friendly people. We turned in our rental car and Jason left to take a train back to Bregenz. We had planted seeds of a friendship with Wolfgang and would visit him later in the States. He is still a Facebook friend and I hear from him on birthdays and holidays. He now lives in Thailand with his wife, Chee and a daughter, Vanessa.

After we were seated for the trip home, the usual announcements were made by our stewardess about safety and emergency protocol. When we became airborne, our pilot announced flight time to Dulles and suggested we set our watches back to US time. It was now 9:00 A.M. Zurich time, 3:00A.M. in the eastern U.S. It actually took nine hours to fly from Zurich to Dulles in Washington D.C. Our flight path took us north over England, Scotland, and in a downward arch over the eastern coast of Canada. We were also traveling against the gulf stream. It was a beautiful, cloudless day, bright with sunshine and miles of ocean, and lands spread before us. I was surprised that I could see land almost all the way. It was a pleasant trip, a bit sad because we were going home, but happy too for exactly the same reason. We both were looking forward to seeing our children and other family. We had some memorable experiences and looked forward to telling our tales back home.

We landed in Washington shortly after noon, back in the good old USA. We were in Washington a couple of hours; cleared customs and caught our flight to Atlanta. From Atlanta we flew Air-South to Columbia arriving late at night due to the inevitable layovers between flights in Washington D.C. and Atlanta. Mom and Dad Widener picked us up in Columbia. By the time we got home it was midnight. We had been up almost 24 hours and were dog tired, but happy to be home. Jet lag is a real drain on the body. I recall feeling so tired I was actually 'limp as a dishrag', as my Grandma would say. My head lolled back and forth on the car seat with every stop and turn of the car. When we pulled up in the yard, it took supreme effort to even get out of the car. Collapsing on the bed, suitcases were just brought inside, no unpacking tonight.

***

Jimmy and I are nowhere near seasoned travelers, but have been fortunate to see places and meet people we never thought possible. Every journey was an adventure. Spring in Austria has been my favorite. Beauty beyond compare, wonderful food, and congenial people.

35. Small World Connection Stories

> "Ships that pass in the night...only a signal shown
> and a distant voice in the darkness; So, on the ocean
> of life, we pass and speak to one another, Only a
> look and a voice, then darkness again and silence"
> —*Henry Wadsworth Longfellow*

It's a small world after all; connections to our fellow men and women are all around us. This is about these connections, so unexpected, that we encounter at the most improbable times and in the most unlikely locations.

Many of us can remember the feelings we have when we connect past experiences through a sense triggered by sight, sound, smell, touch, or taste. It can be triggered by any of our senses. I smell a sweet rose and immediately think of a rose bush that stood beside the porch door in my youth. I hear a voice, perhaps a Southern accent when hundreds or even thousands of miles from home or the crinkling sound of taffeta immediately has brought to mind the crinolines worn in my youth underneath full-skirted dresses. The smooth touch of velvet might bring to mind the soft feel of an evening dress once worn or the fluffy fur of a small kitten caressed in my arms. Then there is taste, sweet, sour, bitter, or salty. I still think of my childhood when I have grits with cheese or have a bitter pill to swallow. I have experienced these memory triggers all my life and have met interesting people far from home that I have some common connection with, that's what these short memories are about. Connections. Not only our senses make a connection to fellow human beings, but conversations play a big part. Everybody has a story and I love to hear them.

When I attended Daughters of the American Revolution Continental Congress in Washington D.C. I found a lot of connections with other folks from across our country. People have picked up on my accent and when I tell them where I'm from, I have been amazed, lots of people have been to the Masters in Augusta or have some family connection to South Carolina. I have found conversations with strangers can become really interesting. Once, I recall, I took an empty seat on the metro in Washington D.C. beside a young black woman. Striking up a conversation has always been easy for me. Within five minutes she told me she was from Ridge Spring, South Carolina, not twenty-five miles away from my home. We didn't have a lengthy conversation, I had to get off at the next station, but there was a connection, all the same.

* * *

My son, Jason, went to Austria to study abroad when he was in college. He had never flown before, but had been accepted to a study abroad program through the University of Illinois in Carbondale. When he arrived in Zurich, Switzerland, he, finally, with his limited German, convinced a taxi driver to take him to his hotel where he had previously secured a reservation. He said, "I got to my hotel room and said aloud to myself, 'what in the hell am I doing here, four thousand miles from home, can't speak the language and don't know a soul.'" He had two nights in Zurich before taking a train to his destination, Bregenz, Austria. The next morning when he went down to the hotel lobby, he heard that Southern accent. He approached strangers, introducing himself, and met a couple from Texas. He made a connection that eased his mind.

He made a life-long friend, Wolfgang Winkler, that fall session of 1994. They met in a bar in Bregenz. When he went back for the Spring session in 1996, Jason lived with Wolfgang, staying in his extra bedroom.

In April of that year, Jimmy and I flew to Austria to stay with Wolfgang in his apartment and visited Jason. While we were there, Wolfgang decided to have a party. He made a big pot of chili and invited some of his friends. We had a wonderful time. Although most of his friends did not speak English, alcohol and real Cuban cigars helped the party become a success. The one thing that impressed me: one of the friends, named Alex, decided to entertain us playing the guitar and singing. Alex could not speak English; however, he played Memphis by Johnny Rivers and sang the whole song in English, every word. That was amazing to me. Jason said Alex was a big fan of Elvis and I have no doubt; he could sing Elvis songs in English too.

* * *

One of Jason's classmates from Austria, Karen, had a brief encounter with someone in Chicago. Karen, a native of Minnesota was visiting friends in Chicago. Stopping at a bar, mostly searching for a restroom, when exiting the restroom, she heard a familiar voice. Approaching a group of guys, she told one guy, "You sound just like my friend, Jason."

"Where is this Jason from?"

"Well," Karen replied, "I met Jason at school in Bregenz, Austria, but he's from South Carolina."

"You must have a good ear for accents," the guy remarked with a grin. "I'm from Columbia, South Carolina." They chatted briefly and parted company, another connection far from home.

* * *

After graduating from college, Jason, made several trips to Europe and Wolfgang has remained a friend. He bought a home outside of Atlanta and lived there with his wife, Chee, from Thailand. Wolfgang was in charge of Quality Assurance at several plants for a company called Alpha. This company makes plastic bottles of every kind all over the world. He was working in Atlanta at one point and lived there. One weekend Jimmy and I, along with Jason and his wife, Vanessa, visited. I like to refer to this visit as an international meeting. Wolfgang, from Austria, Chee from Thailand and son Jack, a couple from Great Britain, husband, wife and daughter, Bethume, Jason's wife, Vanessa, from Peru and of course, we three Americans, Jimmy, Jason, and me. Different cultures, different languages, one connection. Austria, Thailand, Great Britain, Peru, and America all represented, connected by friendship.

* * *

In 2004, we traveled to Canada with friends, Ernie and Pat. Landing in Seattle we rented a car, followed the Okanogan Valley north, crossed the Canadian border and drove the Columbian Icefields Highway as far as Jasper, Alberta. At one overlook, we stopped to take in the majestic Canadian Rockies, glaciers creeping down from the higher altitudes, bright sunshine and pleasant temperatures. A young couple stopped, the guy had on a Clemson cap, Jimmy was wearing a cap with a palmetto tree, South Carolina's state emblem, and orange tiger paw on the back. They, of course, talked and we were face to face with a Clemson graduate way up North in the Canadian Rockies. Small world.

* * *

In 2005, my two sisters, their husbands, my daddy, momma, Jimmy, and I climbed into a fifteen-passenger van, traveled six thousand miles round trip across this great country and returned home in fifteen days. It was a fantastic adventure.

At one point, we found ourselves in Cody, Wyoming at the Sunrise Motor Inn. This was a two-night-stay, so we could relax. When we arrived, Jimmy immediately spotted a car with a South Carolina tag. The car was backing out of a parking space when Jimmy tapped on the window. The couple inside looked dubious at this stranger, but the man rolled down his window.

Jimmy said, "I noticed your South Carolina tag, we're from South Carolina too. Where do you live?"

The man replied, "We live in Easley, South Carolina."

Our daughter, Melanie and her husband, Bill Garrison, lived nearby Easley in Liberty, South Carolina. Of course, these folks knew Bill's parents, in fact were close friends. So here we are in Cody, Wyoming, over two thousand miles from home, talking to a couple of complete strangers who know our daughter's in laws as friends back home in South Carolina. It is a small world.

* * *

My final, ultimate small world connection story was experienced by my son Jason. His first wife, Anastasia, from Greece, and Jason took a ferry from Kalamata, Greece to the island of Crete. On Jason's first trip to Crete, they met a guy named Nikos, who worked for the Port Authority. They became friends and discovered a special bond. Jason and Nikos were born the same day, July 18th, same year, 1973, and at the same time, 5:00 A.M. (of course Nikos was born eight hours earlier because of the time zone difference). An added bonus to this small world connection, Nikos had a sister, three years older, born on July 12, 1970, the same day and year as Jason's sister, Melanie. I met Nikos when I went to Crete myself, but the connection with Jason was undeniable. How many people connect with someone, born the same year, day, and time? Highly unlikely I would guess, especially five thousand miles from home.

My experiences with small world connections make me feel that no matter where or how far from home or comfort zone, there is always a surprise to be found. Smile and say hello to strangers standing in line at the grocery store, drug store, or passing on the sidewalk. You never know when you can make an emotional connection that changes another human being's outlook from depression to joy; sometimes all it takes is a smile and a kind word.

36. Summer of 1999 – Love and Lost

"It was the best of times; it was the worst of times."
— *Charles Dickens*

"A time to weep, and a time to laugh; a time to mourn, and a time to dance."
— *Ecclesiastes 3 verse 4 The Holy Bible*

The above quotes describe, better than I, what June 1999 became to our family. I'll go back a month to set the stage of that fateful month and year. Our daughter, Melanie, was eight months into a difficult pregnancy with our first grandchild. She had developed painful and dangerous blood clots in the thigh of her right leg. Her doctor prescribed total bed rest, staying as immobile as possible. I spent most of the month of May with her. She lived in the upstate of South Carolina in the small town of Liberty with her husband, Bill. I spent a lot of that month taking care of her, so she could stay in bed or recline on the sofa, Bill had to work during the week. I fixed her meals and carried them to her while she rested. I took over their household chores so she could follow her doctor's orders, driving her to doctor's appointments in nearby Greenville.

Kathy Widener

* * *

In May my mother-in-law, Peggy, was on a two-week driving tour out west with her daughter and granddaughter. J.A., my father-in-law was a real homebody and had no wish to accompany them on the trip so he stayed at home. Some nights, Paige, our youngest daughter, would spend the night with Grandpa J.A. just to keep him company.

One-night in late May, Paige called, "Papa had a bad dream, and woke up crying, please come over here."

When Jimmy and I arrived, he was very distraught, but had no physical pain. We stayed a while, bringing him cool, wet wash-cloths to bathe his brow.

"Y'all can go home, I'll be fine," he told us.

A few days later the travelers came home. He seemed his old self, but not for long. Most weekends Jimmy and I were in Liberty and we were there the last Sunday in May 1999 when we received a call. Papa J.A., had become disorientated and an ambulance was requested to transport him to the hospital. He was admitted. Thinking that he may have a kidney infection, he was prescribed the antibiotic, Levaquin, had an allergic reaction, and spent one night in intensive care. Discharged from the ICU to a regular room, Dr. Haas ordered some tests, one was a CAT scan. On Wednesday, June 2nd, the tests were evaluated. Dr. Haas delivered the results.

They were devastating.

"Mr. Widener, you have cancer. Melanoma. It has metastasized and is in your brain, kidneys, bladder, basically everywhere. There is no treatment. We can give radiation and slow the spread, but that is all we can do."

That afternoon, I had to tell Jimmy about the results. That was not easy. He and his father were very close. J.A. was a deacon in the church, loved his family and spoiled his grandchildren. He always kept the nursery at church along with his friend, James. They both were favorites of all the children in church, mainly because they were kind and always had pockets full of candy to give to the children. My father-in-law was a wonderful person, hardworking and loved by all. He could get angry, but he never held a grudge and could get over a hurt easily, never mentioning the problem again. When he worked on any machinery, Jimmy said, "He always had spare parts left over when the job was finished." He was not the best at organization or taking care of tools. They were often left on the ground beside where he worked.

Once he was having a difficult time fixing a push lawnmower. He had reached his limit of patience, said a few well-chosen words, stood and stomped the lawnmower, breaking it into several pieces. Jimmy remembered, he was calm and in a good mood the rest of the day. He took all his anger and frustration out on the lawnmower, not on his loved ones. That was his personality. He was a good and decent Godly man.

* * *

In the meantime, Melanie was experiencing such a difficult pregnancy, she was forbidden to travel and had not seen her Grandpa J.A. since March. He was diagnosed on Wednesday June 2, 1999. That night Jimmy stayed with his dad in the hospital. I went to Burger King and brought them each a Whopper, fries, and a milkshake. I gave both of them a kiss on the cheek that night, and went home to sleep.

The next morning at 5 A.M., I climbed into my car for the long two-and-a-half-hour drive to Liberty, SC. I had to be there at 8

A.M. to carry Melanie to a doctor's appointment. I had no intention of telling her the news about her grandpa. Jimmy was coming for the weekend and we would both tell her then.

The following Saturday evening, we sat on a church pew on their front porch and told Melanie about her Grandpa. She burst into to tears, knowing she could not go home to see him. The next day, he called and talked to Melanie a long time. He told her goodbye, never expecting to see her again in this world.

Melanie was scheduled to be induced on Tuesday, June 8th. That was her Papa J.A.'s birthday and she so wanted to give him his first great grandchild on that day. She was in labor from noon on the 8th until the early hours of June 9th. I was there with her. Jimmy joined Bill and his parents in the waiting room down the hall from labor and delivery. Bill would float in and out of Melanie's room, standing in front of the TV, not knowing what, if anything, he could do.

Every contraction showed the pain on her face, straining to push and breathing in short panting puffs as a nurse sat beside her instructing her how to respond. I stayed, fed her ice chips, and held her hand as each pain consumed her body. Finally, the nurse announced she had dilated enough to receive the shot that would alleviate her pain. A sigh of relief slipped from her lips, knowing an anesthesiologist was on the way. The doctor came to give her a spinal epidural and assured me I was welcome to stay. Big mistake! They sat Melanie up on the edge of the bed and the doctor carefully inserted a needle, which looked to be three inches long into to her spine. I felt faint and retreated to the waiting room. Telling Jimmy, "I have to go outside and get some fresh air now." I'm sure I was white as a sheet. He took me down to the first floor and out into the night air. I sat on the ground and leaned against the warm brick building. There was a slight cool breeze blowing, security lights beamed around the perimeter, the sound of traffic and the swaying of trees against the sky. I began to feel better.

Returning to the vigil in the maternity wing we were told the birth was eminent. Bill was called to the bedside. With a video camera he filmed Emily as soon as she appeared. We four grandparents were waiting outside in the hallway and heard her first cry. Shortly we were allowed inside to see our granddaughter. Bill was holding her, wrapped in the same receiving blanket still used in most hospitals, white with two blue and two pink stripes on one end.

Bill passed Emily to me and the feeling of holding that precious baby, my first grandchild, was indescribable. The closest word I can think to describe the feeling is euphoric, maybe ecstatic, elated, enraptured, or exhilarated. All of the words rolled into one. I would have gladly laid down my life for that little bundle of joy then and there. It was my first grandchild, I loved my children unconditionally, but this was something different. We took turns holding her, gazing into that tiny little face, before leaving to get breakfast and some sleep.

Jimmy called his daddy at about 4:00 A.M to give him the news. Papa J.A. didn't even say hello when he picked up the phone. He simply said, "Do I have a little great granddaughter yet?"

Melanie had more trouble and had to return to the hospital after going home. J.A. returned to the hospital on Tuesday, June 15th. The doctors told Jimmy and the family he would possibly live three months, but that was not God's plan. I took Melanie to a doctor on that Tuesday in Greenville then left for Aiken to be with Jimmy. Arriving at the hospital at 8:50 P.M., I went straight upstairs to Papa J.A.'s room on the third floor. The room and hallway were standing room only. Papa J.A. was laying in the bed, in a coma-like state with a breathing tube inserted in his nose. Jason sat at the head of his granddaddy's bed holding his hand.

When I arrived, I went in and sat on Jimmy's knee. There were people from the church, family, and friends. Here lay a man who had a profound effect on a lot of lives and it was apparent in the faces of those surrounding his bedside. Charmayne, Jimmy's sister, was prepared to spend the night and had brought belongings to stay. Around 9:20, his labored breathing became calmer, opened his eyes for a few seconds, the color drained from his face and he passed away. He never got to hold that precious baby girl. He did get to see pictures of her and a video but he was gone only two weeks after his diagnosis.

* * *

His death was mourned by all who knew him. The next evening, Wednesday, June 16, we had a deluge of rain. We had been suffering from a terrible drought for weeks, grass dry as a bone, dusty roads, even the leaves on trees beginning to turn brown because of the lack of rain. The drought was broken that night with the downpour we received, God in heaven blessed us with his tears to ease our suffering. We all agreed Papa J.A. had put in a special request on our behalf. Of course, we had arrangements to be made for the funeral. Mountains of food and visitors descended on Peggy and J.A.'s home. Jimmy and I also had to find room for an overflow of food and flowers. Visitation was on Thursday night and the line of people waiting to pay tribute to him and his family seemed never ending. We placed a picture of Emily in his inside coat pocket.

It was so sad to lose him, the saddest of all was that he never got to hold his first great grandchild and that Melanie could not be with the family. She could not travel that far and it was a long time before she could even bring herself to visit his grave.

Papa J.A. is in heaven. Never did he profess to be perfect, none of us are, but he was kind to everyone he met and his life meant something special to many people. I believe he watches over his great granddaughter, Emily, and all of us still. I also believe God gave us that precious baby girl, so that during our time of mourning, we also felt great joy that fateful June of 1999.

37. Into the Twenty-first Century

The first decade of the twenty-first century was upon us. People were fearful of Y2K as the transition to a new century was called. Especially, on New Year's Eve, December 31, 1999, many people were apprehensive. The fear mostly sprang from what would happen with all our computer systems. There were many people afraid to fly because computers controlled so much of our lives, what would happen when a new century arrived. Being fearful was a normal reaction, the date change from 1999 to 2000, could cause systems to crash, many believed. Johnny Cash asked a good question in his song, "Where did the twentieth century go?" It did go around like a revolving door; time passes so fast.

The first part of a new century was very dramatic for our country. On September 11, 2001 our country was attacked by terrorists. Four of our own planes were commandeered by these terrorists, flights taken over by radicals at Logan Airport in Boston. The attack was planned and executed by middle eastern men that flew two planes into the Twin Towers in New York City, crashed a plane into the Pentagon, and attempted to crash another into a Washington D.C. target. The fourth plane was taken back by brave Americans that refused to go down without a fight. It crashed before their evil objective could be completed, in a field in Shanksville, Pennsylvania. All on board were killed.

In February 2001, our grandson, Tristen, was born, the son of our daughter, Paige. She and Tristen's father had addiction problems and after less than a year, their demands, which we could not meet, caused an estrangement between us and them. We were not allowed to see our grandson for over five years. Most of that time we had no idea where they were or what had become of Tristen. All we could do was pray. In 2008, Tristen was placed in foster care. Jimmy and I became foster parents and the Department of Social Services placed him in our home in May of 2009. I believe his parents loved him, it was more a case of neglect and discord between his parents. There was a lot of involvement with law enforcement and the use of drugs. In October 2011, Jimmy and I became his adoptive parents. Now in our old age, we are again parents of a ten-year-old.

38 Daddy Could Tell Stories Too

I gave my daddy a journal for Christmas 2012. He had passed his eighty-ninth birthday in November. He was pretty frail, but his mind was still sharp. His handwriting was pretty slow and a little squiggly, almost like a person who suffers from tremors.

"Daddy, whenever you are sitting in your cushioned rocker and a memory comes to mind, please write it down," I told him. He didn't fill the pages, but what he wrote were about things I had never heard before. Keep in mind he was born in 1923. The following is in his own words:

"In my early years I had no one my age to play with. It happened that daddy's brother, Rion, and his family lived right across the branch from us and they had 5 girls, so we played together a lot.

When I got a little older, they moved away and I got big enough to visit with a family that lived up the hill from us. They had 2 boys about my age and we played together a lot. One time we were going to build a mountain with a wheelbarrow. That didn't last long. So, then we were going to make a railroad from their house down to our house, but that didn't work too well. So, we dug us a cave in the ground and covered it over with small trees, but the family made us fill it in with dirt.

When Highway 178 was built, Mr. Reedy Gunter bought a

dump truck and hauled cement to help build the road. They moved to North, S.C. and later they moved to Chester, S.C. to help build roads. This happened before Mr. Reedy's sons, Drayton, J.E. and I started the mountain and the railroad.

Our next project was to build a log cabin. We cut down oak logs and made the cabin, got bricks and made a fireplace to it. We had a wood floor and dug a cellar in it.

When I got a litter older so I could walk down to Rayflin by myself, I started going down there to play with Uncle Roston and Aunt Jennie's children. That is when the Swamp Rabbit train was through there. When I got older, Cora Lee and Edith (Roston's girls) would comb and make waves in my hair. We had lots of fun playing games.

The Swamp Rabbit Railroad was built in from Seivern to Batesburg in 1898, and was built to haul chalk mainly. It also hauled pulpwood and crossties from Rayflin at times. There was a shack there too. If passengers wanted to board, you got out on the track and waved the train so they would stop to pick you up. There was a black man who lived across the branch from us at that time. He had been to Wagener and I saw him get off of the train with his guitar and drum. His name was Will Smith.

In about 1931 or 1932 the chalk mine had closed down and there were not enough things to haul, so the railroad quit running, and was torn up about 1933. Most people at that time hated to see the railroad torn up. Daddy's brother, Roston Gantt, ran a store in Rayflin, and lots of produce was sent by rail. Coca Cola came in big wooden crates. Later on, a truck brought Coca Cola there in small 24 bottle crates. I don't remember what year, but not many years later he closed the store, when the depression came in the Hoover days. My Grandaddy, J.K. Gantt, had 504 acres of land, had a stroke in 1927.

Every Life Tells a Story

After he had the stroke, he could not get over his place good enough to find things like he wanted to. He could walk some, but could not talk much. I was old enough to remember him then. He passed away in 1930. After then is when a lot of liquor making went on.

Grandaddy was a strong man. It was said that he could stand in a half bushel measure and put a 200-pound sack of fertilizer on his shoulder.

During the depression years, a lot of fishing and opossum hunting went on. I remember we had a bulldog named Sadie and she would tree possums. One night when daddy and Leon were hunting, she found a skunk on the ground and the dog killed it. They told me where it was, so me and the 2 boys (Drayton and J.E Gunter) that lived up the hill decided to skin the skunk and sell the hide. Boy that was a job. We had a time getting that smell off of us. We skinned it wrong and could not sell the hide.

When I was in grammar school, I could buy a loaf of bread or a big cinnamon roll for 5 cents. When I got my first car, I could buy 5 gallons of gas for 95 cents. During World War II you had to have stamps to buy gas, shoes, sugar, and lots of other things like tires. Car companies didn't make cars from 1942 until 1945, they made war vehicles. Times were tough in Depression years and war years. You were lucky to get a job for 50 cents or $1.00 a day for 10 hours work. The President started up a WPA NYA and CCC camps and things began to get a little better, thank the Lord. After the War was over in 1945, things got better and you could get a job pretty easy.

During the War years as a teenager on weekends, I would go out around Fairview to be with other boys my age that I knew. Sometimes we went possum hunting. One night I walked home by myself from Mrs. Beulah Rogers' house.

Back in the early 1930's airplanes were very few. If one came over and you heard it you would jump up and run out to see it. One day down at Uncle Roston's store one came over and they had been talking about carrying the mail by air. There were several women out in the yard looking at it. One of them said, "That might be a mail plane." Uncle Roston replied, "Male plane, Hell, that is them wheels you see hanging down under there."

One day when the railroad was still running, Daddy was walking up the railroad to Steadman and he heard something in the leaves making a noise and he looked and it was a king snake and a rattlesnake all wound up together. He said he had always heard that a king snake would kill other snakes, so he left them to see when he came back, and sure enough when he came back the dead rattlesnake was there and the king snake was gone."

My Daddy passed away on a bright Sunday morning, February 22, 2015. He was a wonderful father and I was so truly blessed by his presence. Everyone who knew him admired him. He was kind and generous and taught me what is important in life.

39. She's Gone Now

Her name was Sallie Elizabeth, named for both her grandmothers. I always thought the Elizabeth part was the prettiest name, but she was called Sallie by family and friends. My siblings and I called her momma. She passed from this world Monday, May 6, 2019 about five in the evening. My oldest sister, Louise, sat beside her bed, holding her hand and speaking quietly to her. Of course, there was no response from Momma Sallie, but at least she had company when she crossed over. She was eighty-eight years old.

Louise said, "I could feel the presence of three angels at the head of the bed as momma slipped away." She always seemed to have a bit of a connection to things supernatural, a phenomenal link to the unseen that surround us.

Momma Sallie had been in nursing facilities for the last ten years. I had not visited her for at least four years. There was a reason for the distance and I am writing this to explain not so much for others to hear, but for myself. She abandoned me and my siblings when I was six years old, but that had nothing to do with me not having contact with her. That was sixty years ago and I have long forgiven her for her actions. She was very young, only fifteen, when she married my daddy. At the time, I believe, she married him to escape what had become for her almost enslavement. She lived with her Grandma Lizzie, her father's mother, and did all the chores. Grandma Lizzie had two girls, one a mongoloid child, the other married. There were at least four boys at home. Sallie was sent to help Grandma Lizzie; she was expected to do all the cooking, washing clothes, and cleaning for Lizzie, husband Milledge, their sons and Dempsey, their special needs daughter. Momma said she was so young she had to stand on a chair to wash dishes, iron clothes, and cook. She had no childhood.

My daddy, I'm sure, was an appealing alternative. He was quiet and shy and treated her well. They married in May 1945, then along came us kids. The first child momma delivered was stillborn, a son, delivered at home by Miss Willow. That had to be a hard to accept for a sixteen-year-old mother. Daddy received a certificate from the coroner to bury the child himself. There was no funeral, just daddy and Mr. Reedy Gunter, a small wooden coffin daddy built that he and Mr. Reedy buried in the Pine Grove church cemetery. There is a granite tombstone, Robert Kelly Gantt Jr. July 2nd 1946. In 1947, she had Louise, then Lula Mae, me, and Steve. She had reasons to want to free herself from her responsibilities and I never held her decision to leave against her, certainly not now.

Was there ever a time when I felt we were mother and daughter? What kind of person was she? Both these questions I have been pondering and felt the need to spill words onto paper, thinking it would fill the emptiness of our relationship.

After momma left, we seldom had any contact with her, at least until our teen years. She and my daddy were legally divorced when I was in fifth grade. Daddy remarried and momma floated in and out of my life. Momma Sallie also remarried to Palmon Spires. He got in trouble with the law for selling moonshine. One of his customers, so momma said, was a judge. This judge told Palmon never to get caught and appear in his court, if he did, he would be sent to jail. That's exactly what happened. He did time for two years. Palmon turned out to be a good man and became an ordained minister, serving many years in that capacity. I feel sure Momma Sallie had many men friends before and after she met Palmon. She was an attractive woman and very intelligent, although she did not have much formal education. Momma and Palmon had a son, L.P. Jr. He was born in April 1964, before I even met Jimmy.

She never attended any of our band concerts, ballgames, or even our high school graduations that I can remember. She was a hardworking person, loved working in the yard, and could be very entertaining. When I started dating Jimmy, we would visit her, Palmon, and L.P. She was a good cook and was happy to have us come. She never smelled of alcohol or smoked. She did keep a jug of moonshine in her hall closet with peppermint candy in it to dose L.P when he had a bad cough. A tablespoon of that pink fiery elixir would not only cure his cough, I'm sure it momentarily took his breath away. He didn't dare cough in Momma's presence if he could restrain the urge.

If he did, Momma would loudly say, "Come here L.P. right now, let me give you something to shut up that cough." He would respond to her call, dragging his feet all the way. He knew what to expect. A tablespoon of peppermint moonshine worked wonders on a cough.

Just like all people she had her faults, some that finally became too much for me and my brother to bear. After we graduated from high school and became adults, we saw her pretty often. She and Palmon came to my wedding and paid for the photographer. I actually lived with her and L.P, when Jimmy was in the Army and I was pregnant with my first child. Palmon worked for years in Baxley, Georgia, only coming home on the weekends, so I stayed with her.

Momma came and spent the night with us sometimes and she could be very entertaining. Sometimes we would play Canasta or gin rummy, her favorite card games, or she would regale us with stories of our kin folks, some I hesitate to mention. She knew all the skeletons in everybody's closet, trust me we all have a few. Once she came for an overnight stay bringing her gown and necessities in a big brown paper bag and sat it down by the backdoor. At that time, there were no fenced recycle stations to take trash, bottles, and cans to be disposed of, however there were three dumpsters down the road from our house. Jimmy got all the trash together and took it to the dumpsters soon after momma arrived. When bed time came, guess what, her bag was gone. Thinking it was trash, Jimmy took it to the dumpster. We drove to dumpsters, taking a flashlight to help in the search. Sure enough, her bag of clothes was found, at least we didn't have to climb into the dumpster to retrieve them. On one visit, she sat in one of the antique wooden chairs at our kitchen table and it completely splintered into a dozen or more pieces. She was sitting flat on the floor, the chair in pieces all around her. She wasn't hurt, but Jimmy said, "I hope you're not going to sue us." Her reply, "That's what you buy homeowners insurance for isn't it?" She didn't sue us, but I was concerned.

Momma could be a vindictive person and always ready to pay someone back for wrongs directed at her. After she and Palmon divorced, split the sheets, her terminology, there were many other men friends. One was Louise's age and when he and momma broke up, she was so angry, it was told she planted drugs in his car then turned him in to the law. Another payback she purportedly suggested for wrongs, was pour sugar in the gas tank of their car, completely destroys the engine. She also was rumored to have set at least three homes afire to collect the insurance money, none could be proven. I did hear her say, "Just put some grease in a frying pan, turn on the stove, and walk out the door."

She spent lots of money on clothes, and anything else she saw that she wanted. She was good at beating the system, once I was in JB Whites in Aiken and I saw her taking clothes off racks and piling them on the desk surrounding the cash register. I just watched her; she didn't see me. She kept taking clothes off racks and depositing them beside the register, never trying on any of them. That piqued my curiosity. I walked to the register to pay for a blouse. Standing right beside her, she never noticed me until I spoke, she was too intent on picking out clothes. We spoke briefly and she gave me a hug. I later found out; momma was declaring bankruptcy so she was maxing out her credit card before filing. Very adapted at getting what she wanted, she collected food stamps, SSI payments, and heaven only knows what else from the government.

I don't remember what she and Steve really fell out over, except I know she wanted something, another car, I think. Anyway, she called him. "I think my children should pay for it," she stated on the phone. When he told her no way, he couldn't buy her a car, she hung up. He promptly called her back and hung up on her. When he did speak to her, he told her, "Now you know what it's like for someone to hang up on you." Her reply, "I don't want you to even come to my funeral." Steve said, "Be careful what you ask for."

Steve just had back surgery, attended the funeral in a wheel chair, but did come.

The thing that really 'was the straw that broke the camel's back' for me was the horrible accusation against my daddy, saying he tried to sexually assault her. Anyone who has ever known my daddy could vouch that there was no way that was true. She would say completely wild things, even once said Grandma Florence was burning in Hell. Wanting a new mobile home, she called daddy, told him she had worked in a sewing room and bought part of the blocks he used to build his house and he should be willing to co-sign for her to get it. After saying those things, I no longer felt obligated to have any contact with her. She was a self-centered person and always put herself above others. I don't mean to speak ill of the dead, but I had too much going on in my life and refused to deal with her nonsense. Her whole life as long as she was able was truly like a Jerry Springer Show. I couldn't deal with that any longer.

My two sisters, Louise and Lu, visited momma and Louise saw to her care. Maybe Louise remembered her as a better mother, she is four years older than me. I have long forgiven her for things she has done. She did carry me for nine months and gave me life. I pray that her soul is at peace in heaven, but I also believe, it was God's will that she left us kids with daddy and grandma. My daddy had a happy life with my stepmother for over fifty-two years before he died in 2015.

Momma's funeral was held on Friday and there were a lot of people there. I believe she is in heaven now. Her pastor said, "You never knew what was going to come out of her mouth." But he visited her and asked her if she was saved.

"Don't lie to me now, Miss Sallie, I want the truth." Pastor Padgett insisted.

Momma told the pastor, "I have done a lot of things I am ashamed of, but yes I have asked forgiveness and I am saved."

I pray for her soul and that at last she will rest in peace.

I guess most everybody has a family member they have to love from afar. I loved momma, but for my own peace of mind and sanity, it had to be at a distance during her last years.

40. Glimpses of a Life Well Lived

Lives are defined by heightened senses and small memories. A word, a song, a smell can bring a special memory to mind. Like a blinding flash, a memory pops into your mind. Sometimes happy. Sometimes sad.

I have special moments that run through my mind, especially when I sit, gaze out my window, watch the rain pour from the roof, or on a sunny day a gentle breeze tip toeing across the highest limbs of the giant oaks in my backyard. Sometimes my mind seems to work stranger than most. I ponder the times of my life, things I have experienced through my senses.

I have walked on a glacier in the Canadian Rockies. Laughed with my sisters until it hurt. I have flown across the Atlantic twice and connected with people from foreign lands. I have listened to their stories and they to mine. Heard and seen the thundering waters of Niagara Falls dropping over the precipice above. Toured Washington D.C. where a kindly old gentleman put a new role of film into my complicated camera. I have met with smiles when asking perfect strangers to please hand me something from a top shelf in a grocery store out of my reach. A smile and polite manner do wonders. Cradled innocent babies in my arms and heard peals of laughter from a baby that had yet to utter their first word. The laughter sparked simply by a game of peek a boo. That, I believe, is the sweetest sound in the world, a baby's laughter. I have stood beside a crib and saw my grandchild sucking her thumb.

Traveled across our great country by plane several times, once 6,000 miles round trip in a fifteen-passenger van. Stood at the edge of the Grand Canyon, posed with a Park Ranger at the base of Mt. Rushmore in South Dakota. Visited the famed Deadwood and the final resting place of Wild Bill Hickok. I have watched the sunset over the river swamp behind dark sentinels of junipers, saw the sunset over the ocean, imagining a sizzle as it appeared to touch the water at the horizon. I have eaten meals with strangers in Greece, Crete, Austria, and Germany, not understanding their speech but feeling their kindred spirit. Crossed the blue-black waters of the Mediterranean on a ferry boat. Rode at unimaginable speeds on the autobahn in Germany, passed by cars as if we were standing still.

Held a small child's hand crossing the street. Met people far from home who turned out to be kind to a stranger. As a child, spun round and round, arms outstretched until I grew dizzy and fell in a heap on the ground, laughing. Roller skated in my youth at Rainbow Lake. Remember food before fast food chains were in every town and on every street corner in the land, Coca Cola, Pepsi, and Buffalo Rock ginger ale in glass bottles, all costing ten cents each.

Hovered with friends and family around a wood stove in Winter to have a conversation and listened to ghost stories from old folks. I've toured the museums of Washington D.C. Visited the White House. Bought hot dogs and ice creams from street vendors in our nation's Capital and Innsbruck, Austria. Sat in pubs with girlfriends. Ate at a two-story McDonald's dressed in a gold lame evening gown, spaghetti straps, and gold high heeled sandals with friends dressed in evening gowns and tuxedoes. Sailed on cruise ships, once with my husband to Alaska.

I have felt the Spirit of God move in Revival Meetings, where prayer and preaching revived my spirt, clapping and singing elevated my heart and cleansed my soul. The quiet times with my husband, laying in his arms and feeling his love. These are all memories, none more important than the others. My life is comprised of moments. These moments when remembered define a lifetime well lived.

41. Time Passengers

Time is a sneaky bandit. You live your life, working, caught up in the mundane day to day chores. Children involved in school recitals, dance and piano lessons, ball games, and everyday occurrences, doctor and dentist appointments to attend. There are always groceries to buy, meals to cook, and house cleaning that so desperately needs to be done. Time finally catches up with the speed of your life. You realize there are books to be read, conversations to share, and adventures you hope for. Remember when the best times of your life were conversations on the front porch when the weather turns cool or surprise company that just drops by to say hello. Those days seem to be long past. You lose family and friends along the way, by death or complacency. I have found that friendships, like marriages and children, require cultivation and attention. Phone calls are good, but when is the last time you wrote a letter or sent a personally signed card? We all need to slow down and smell the roses.

I well remember sandy dirt roads, no street signs giving them names. Every field, not planted, grown up with broom straw, a little empty rundown shack, tin roof rusty and blown off; there always seemed to be a cedar tree beside the shaky, falling brick chimney. Kudzu vines covered the walls, boards stripped from the sides. This was a tenant house and they were all over in the South of my youth. They are no more. Fields once plowed are grown up in pines, some thirty- or forty-feet high today. The dirt road where we lived now has nice brick homes, air-conditioned, with two or three indoor baths. A cedar tree in my momma's yard, Christmas tree size when I still lived at home is now a huge tree, the base a foot across.

Time robs you of your youth, wrinkles develop, hair turns gray; men and women lose hair where they want it and grow hair where they don't. Skin sags and pounds collect. Gravity takes its toll on our bodies. The world around us has changed, both physically, mentally and I believe, tragically. It was once in vogue to know where you came from, gaze on the likeness of the people who were here generations before. The young people of today know very little of America's history or those revered for their sacrifices on our behalf. The past cannot be undone, we must look to the future, and remember our unique heritage of freedom.

I remembered that blessed freedom watching the changing of the guards at the Tomb of the Unknown Soldier at Arlington National Cemetery. Rows upon rows of white marble gravestones at Arlington, across the Potomac, so many marking the resting place of America's military, many who gave 'the last full measure'.

I was fortunate to grow up with 'the greatest generation'. I remember those who fought to keep us free, both WWI and WWII. I knew many of these men and women. There are very few WWII, Korean, and Vietnam veterans, men and women still alive. How many young people in their late teens or early twenties can tell you who Audie Murphy was, even John Wayne or Jimmy Stewart?

I would venture to say, none can tell you what a catface on a long leaf pine signifies or how to read signs in the forest, moss grows on the north side of a tree. The sun rises in the east and sets in the west. The phrase "riding into the sunset", great cowboy phrase, what does that mean? What is the capital city in the state they live in? They know very little about geography, how the government is supposed to work. They probably know who the U.S. President is now because of the media obsession with President Trump. Do they know who was President when Pearl Harbor was attacked. Where is Pearl Harbor? What was the Doolittle Raid and what a morale booster it was to Americans? Can they even locate the United States on a globe? Can they sign their names in cursive, even read it? We called it real writing in my day.

Everything has changed, not just traditions and values. Animals never seen in my childhood are now abundant: deer, turkey, armadillos, and coyotes that yelp as the darkness caresses the country landscapes. Changes have come, not just to the countryside, but to the cities as well. Pollution hangs a heavy curtain of fog above big cities, noise and chaos reigns in the streets.

Growing up in the 1950's and 60's was indeed a blessing. Cars were much more appealing, maybe not gas efficient, but much prettier with sleek designs and colors, from the hues of an evening sunset to the greens displayed on the forest floor, the canopy above or amazing colors from flowers growing in yards beside the road. I remember from my youth purple irises, flaming red spider lilies, and daylilies in a rainbow of colors. Cars from the 1950's and sixties came in these magnificent colors. Men dressed in suit pants, navy or khaki casuals, long sleeve shirts, ties, and fedora hats. Now any clothing is acceptable, even pajamas are worn in high end department stores and on the streets of cities. Are there still signs on entrance doors that state, 'shirt and shoes required'? I believe the way you dress when in public is a reflection on yourself and your respect for others.

Cars were not merely computers on wheels like today's, any

shade tree mechanic could work on the car's engine. One day you look around. I mean really look at the places you visit and live. Remember how things were when you were young. There was no GPS. All roads looked the same, most were probably not on any map. The map had to be in your head.

Time stops for no man or woman. That is why our memories must be preserved. We need to leave something behind, stories, pictures, and most of all traditions. We are all really time passengers, just here for a brief stay before traveling to another place.

42. Advice From My Lifetime

As I near my seventieth year, I think back on what my life has been. I would venture to say, mine has been a blessed life. Luck had nothing to do with it.

From my days in high school, when I thought I was something special to now, when I know I was never that different from any other teenager in that category. I was certainly raised to be blessed. I had people I could depend on to steer me in the right direction and that loved me unconditionally.

Here are some words of wisdom to help others, if that is possible:

1. Youth is definitely wasted on the young. I never thought I would make it this far. If I had known, I would have enjoyed every day more. I would have slowed down and did what my husband has always done, read every sign in museums and every historical marker by the roadside. Someday you'll look back and regret the rush. You could have gained so much more from the experience if you had taken the time.

2. If a pair of shoes feels comfortable when you put them on, like you could walk all day and not have to stop. Make your feet happy, buy them. I have bought my share of uncomfortable shoes, because I am a female that loves cute shoes. Cute

shoes or not, I'm too old for high heels, I trip over my own feet. At my age I could easily break a hip. I well remember running down steps and rocky trails, I don't do that now. I have learned caution.

3. If you have really good friends, you have been blessed. I'm talking about friends you can call at 3:00 a.m. and they will come. When our youngest child was found dead in a locked room, the good Lord had planned that for minimum distress, if there is any such thing. Both of our older children were home for the weekend when we got the call that Saturday morning in May. She was living in a home on York Street for women who had need of help with addictions, called Stand at the Crossroads Ministry. Miss Debbie, the founder, called. She asked to speak to Jimmy. Paige had been found unresponsive and an ambulance was on the way. Jimmy told me, "You stay here, I'll call you."

Though he protested, our daughter, Melanie, a registered nurse, insisted she was going with him. She later said, "When there was no ambulance on the scene, I knew it was the worse."

She was there to support her Dad and Jason was here to comfort me. We had adopted Paige's son, Tristen, he was a teenager. Jimmy called and told me she was gone, I sobbed with disbelief, Jason stood beside me as I took the call. I could only whisper in a hoarse quiet voice, "How can I tell Tristen?" Even with all the bad memories of his parents, he still loved them. His mother had recently, with God's help, become a different person.

Jason placed his hand on my shoulder, "I'll tell him, Mom" and he disappeared to Tristen's room to give the bad news to a sixteen-year-old young man.

Here's where the good friends come in, my six sister friends went on a junket that Saturday morning, I didn't go. God knew where I needed to be. I called one friend, the one I knew would answer her cell phone. I told her, "Paige has been found dead."

Without any hesitation she replied, "We'll be there in fifteen minutes," and three of them were, they were in the car when I called. They sat with me and just listened as I poured out my grief and shock, tears flowing down my cheeks. Just having them to unload this burden was a balm for my sorrow. That was important. Remember God gave us two ears, just one mouth. We need to listen more than talk.

That was Saturday, May 20, 2017; a sad day for any parent. I always believed children should outlive their parents, but sometimes that is not God's plan. The next six days were a blur. Friends and family came and went, expressing love and filling our home with food and flowers.

We had seen Paige on May 11, met her at Fatz to celebrate Jimmy's birthday. She was all smiles, a different person. We thought she would make it this time.

A quote from Dr. Seuss, "Sometimes you will never know the value of a moment until it becomes a memory." That birthday supper was one of those moments. If I had known, I would have hugged her a bit tighter and told her how proud I was of what she was accomplishing, but that is not the way life works.

Paige's Memorial Service was held at Windsor Baptist Church on the following Thursday. The church was packed. We let Tristen make all the decisions as to speaker and music. He went to school every day the week of her passing. He wanted to be with his friends, not a bunch of old people sitting around at home.

Tristen did the eulogy for his mother. I was so proud of him. He did not waver or appear nervous when he stood behind the podium on the pulpit. He even asked Jimmy and me to stand up and spoke of us as his new Momma and Daddy. It so reminded me of a little five-year-old girl who asked the preacher in that same church over thirty years before if she could stand up after the Christmas program and recite the Christmas story, thirteen verses from the book of Luke that she had memorized. Now her sixteen-year-old son was giving her eulogy; he had written himself.

One More Important Piece Of Wisdom.

Always treat everyone the same. Be kind, smile, and say hello whenever you pass a person on the sidewalk, the aisle of the grocery store, or in the checkout line at department stores. You never know what a smile and a kind word can do. I always speak to everyone I meet; I don't care what their gender, skin color, sexual orientation, religion, or lack of might be. I am not anyone's judge. I have had completely marvelous experiences talking to strangers. We can't know what kind of sorrows or problems they have and a kind word from a passing stranger may have an immeasurable effect on someone's life.

We all will be leaving this world one day, we're not immortal. If God knows the number of hairs on my head, "But even the hairs on your head are numbered. Fear not therefore: ye are of more value than many sparrows." (Luke 12:7 Holy Bible) I am sure He knows my departure date. I am thankful for everything God has given me, there are so many millions of people who are starving and have no place to sleep. A good idea to impress on the younger generation that refuse to eat their supper because it's not something they like. In my childhood, parents would say, "Eat your vegetables, there are children starving in Africa" and in America, families living in cars or cardboard boxes. And the young people of this country can complain.

Every Life Tells a Story

* * *

When my life is done, I want people to remember me. Friends and family that smile when they hear my name. I want my stories to cause laughter, not sadness. If I achieve that, I will have been a success in this life. All I care about is the here and now, living life to the fullest and making people smile.

I have seen an intricate spider web, woven to perfection, anchored in several directions. The early morning sun shining through, drops of dew hanging suspended to each delicate strand, marveling in the beauty that took the spider hours to construct. The web becomes invisible with the sun's movement, the dew gone, unwittingly I walk through this creation, destroying it in seconds. The web has to be snatched away so quickly, a natural reflex. It's a creepy feeling to have the web clinging to my body. Is that spider on me or my clothes? Feeling sorry to have destroyed something so amazing is an afterthought.

Life and your memories are like unto the beauty of a spider's web. Remember it only takes seconds for your life to be completely destroyed, your memories gone forever. That is why I have chosen to write them down; the reader would be smart to remember this analogy of the spider's web.

> "Life is all memory, except for the one present moment that goes by you so quickly you hardly catch it going."
> —*Tennessee Williams*

Kathy Widener

"The September of My Years"

One day you turn around, and it's summer
Next day you turn around and it's fall
And the springs and the winters of a life time
Whatever happened to them all?

—Frank Sinatra

DAR pages from SC standing by the Speaker's desk US House of Representatives 1985
L to R—Mary Alice, Brenda, Penny, Kathy (author), and Mary Lou

Every Life Tells a Story

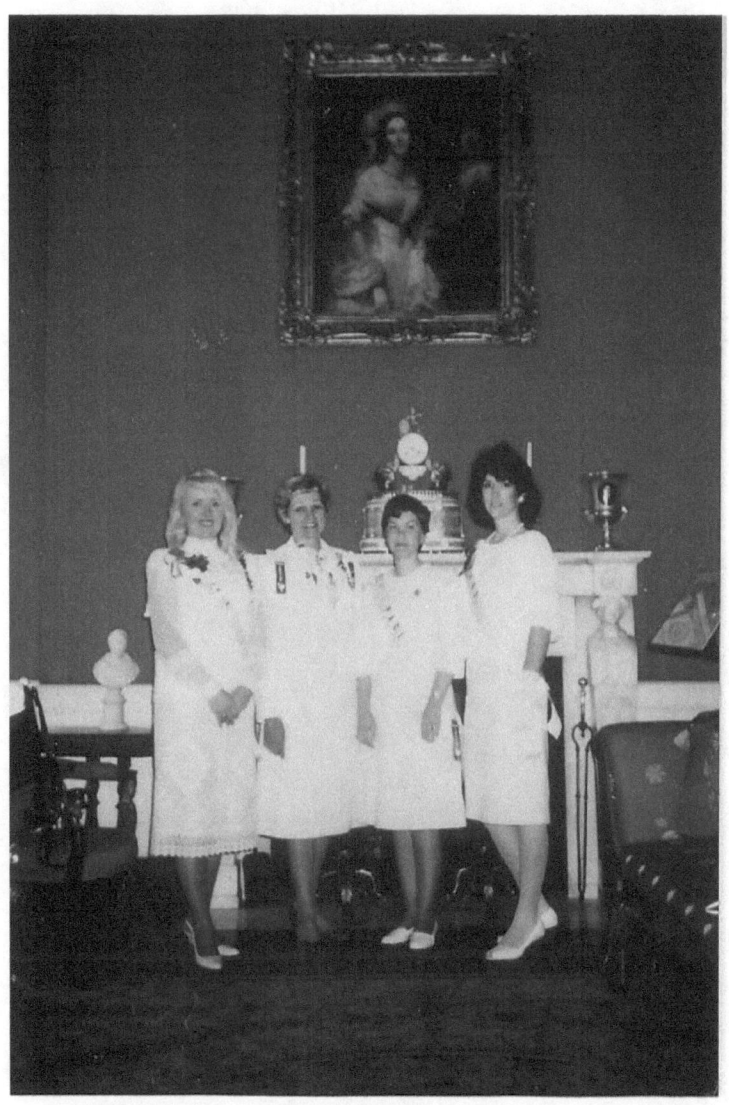

DAR Ladies, Red Room of the White House
L to R— Mary Lou, Nancy, Kathy and Mary Alice

South Carolina State DAR Conference Celebrating a Century of Service to the nation. Kathy G Widener representing the 1920's as a flapper

Every Life Tells a Story

DAR pages at SC state conference in Columbia SC heading to Tea at the Governor's Mansion, Author in the middle

Kathy Widener

Author enjoying a real Cuban cigar in Austria

Every Life Tells a Story

Wolfgang Winkler, Jason Widener and Kathy enjoying an ice cream cone in Innsbruck, Austria April 1996

Jason in foreground outside the Castle in Vaduz, Liechtenstein

Kathy Widener

Jason, Renada (Wolfgang's friend), Wolfgang and Kathy — 'Forest Bar' near Lindau, Germany

Jimmy between the tattoo guy and his friend

Kathy and Jimmy enjoying German beer (not really from these huge mugs)

Enjoying a meal with the Winklers, Wolfgang's parents, at their apartment

Mr. and Mrs. Winkler, our supper hosts, Wolfgang in between

Jason and Kathy climbing the stairs to Waldschenke 'Forest Bar'

Jimmy holding our granddaughter, Emily — June 1999

DAR Luncheon at SC Conference — Esther, Kathy and Brenda

Every Life Tells a Story

DAR Banquet—L to R Esther Cope, Darlene Williams, Senator Thurmond, and Kathy. Group picture imposed over photo of the Capitol on Easter Sunday 1987 (notice the cross made with Easter Lilies on the Capitol steps)

Kathy Widener

Official adoption of our grandson, Tristen Allen Widener, October 26, 2011

Every Life Tells a Story

Official adoption presided over Judge Deborah Neese
L to R — Melanie, Jason, Kathy, Judge Neese, Tristen standing in front
of his Papa Jimmy, Kathy's parents, Robert and Jeanette Gantt

About the Author

Kathy was born in Batesburg, SC, in 1951, the third child of Robert and Sallie Hartley Gantt. She graduated from Pelion High School in 1969 and married Jimmy Widener one month after graduation. They had three children: Melanie, Jason, and Paige. Eighteen years after graduating from high school, Kathy attended USC Aiken, majoring in history. In 1990, she received an Associate in Arts with high honors. College was more for self-gratification than the pursuit of a new career. She became an amateur genealogist in her early twenties and interviewed many older family members, asking questions and taking notes. This, of course, was many years before personal computers and the internet. She always loved stories told by older folks. Their lives and experiences fascinated her. Those stories eventually led to her authorship of three books based on family memories told by elders in her childhood. She remembered cool nights, a heaven of stars, and listening to the past sitting on the front porch. Deciding memories are all important, she wanted them to be preserved and recorded.

www.ingramcontent.com/pod-product-compliance
Lightning Source LLC
Chambersburg PA
CBHW030318100526
44592CB00010B/478